How to Deal with 1

By Dr. P. D. Coker

ISBN 07457 0231 7

How to Deal with Disk Disasters

©1993 Dr. P. D. Coker

Published by:

Kuma Books Ltd
12 Horseshoe Park
Pangbourne
Berks
RG8 7JW

Tel 0734 844335
Fax 0734 844339

CONTENTS

Preface

I've talked to hundreds of computer users over the past few years and I've asked them all the same question.

'What computer problem, apart from viruses, worries you most?'

Almost all, whether they used mainframes or PCs, at work or home, said that data loss was the most significant worry. Further questioning revealed that the particular data-loss problems related to loss of or damage to floppy disks or to the failure of a hard disk.

There were several reasons for writing this book, the most important of which was to put the experience I've gained over to other users, whether they are involved with computers at work or at home. Another reason was the most American books on the subject tended to be over-long and so heavy that they could give you a hernia and a severe pain in the wallet.

I hope that the end result will be useful to all sorts of people, particularly those whose lives have been made miserable by disk problems.

I must thank Rosemary and Bryony for being, respectively, computer widow and semi-orphan - but, more seriously, for being so understanding when the deadline approached. Several friends and colleagues helped in one way or another - in particular, John Kilcline, John Parker and James Rocks who gave generously of their expertise, time and their senses of humour - and sold me a few items as well! I'd also like to thank Chris Robinson for some very useful discussions. Finally, those people at the University of Greenwich whose disk disasters came my way - I won't name them, but some ought to have known better - such as the lecturer who used a floppy disk as a coffee mat or the student whose floppy disk had a brief and unintentional spell as a frisbee, and ended up being chewed by an inquisitive puppy! Sorry, Lisa and Fr.... whoops!

Paddy Coker   Farnborough, August 1993

Introduction

Almost all computer users will, at some time or another, experience a sudden, frequently dramatic but always inconvenient problem with a floppy disk or a hard disk drive.

The scenario might be like this:

You want to look at your client database in order to amend it and carry out a mailshot for your new product range which is far in advance of any of your rivals' and...

or like this:

It's midnight.   You have just carried out a minor edit and spell-check on that 10,000 word report which has to be handed in first thing tomorrow morning.   You start to save it and ...

.... you get a message on screen, such as 'Data error writing drive C'...
.... and the machine locks up!

You try to find your backup disk.   OH NO! - I lent it to my auntie in Heckmondwicke/I've put my mug of scalding hot coffee on it/ the dog's just eaten it/.... I didn't back it up!

What can I do now?

Go out and get drunk? Kick the computer? Kick the cat? File for bankruptcy?

No!   Read the first few chapters of this book - carefully!   It might help - specially the cat!

It's never happened to you? Umm........?

How you can get the best from this book

This book is divided into two parts. The first part is the **essential background to data recovery**, no matter when it strikes.

The first four chapters are designed to give prompt help without too much background.

If something has gone wrong, read **chapter 1 (FIRST AID)** - and take a little time to answer the questions because these might help you or someone else pin-point the problem. **Chapter 2** deals with **HARD DISKS** and should be helpful, even if the problems are pretty severe.

Chapter 3 tells you how to recover from problems if you have a copy of **Norton Utilities** available. Provided the hard disk hasn't seized up, this is one of the easiest ways.

Chapter 4 is for those who, either by accident or design, need to make their recovery using **DOS utilities.**

The next 3 chapters are mainly concerned with getting yourself organised so that you can avoid the worst effects of disk disasters in the future.

Chapter 5 deals with the all-important business of **survival** - and how you can make things easier for yourself - and it's followed by a **warning about elderly DOS**es.

Chapter 7 is all about backing up your disks and related matters.

Part 2 is full of **background** information about operating systems, disks, data storage and diagnostics.

Chapter 8 deals with the various **versions of DOS** and their facilities (or lack of them) and **chapter 9** looks at some of the **commercial disk recovery and repair utilities** which are currently available.

Chapter 10 investigates the **facts and fallacies of disk disasters.**

Chapters 11 and 12 are concerned with the various facets of **data storage** and **how disk drives operate** and **chapter 13** looks specifically at problems which can occur with **floppy disks**. **Chapter 14** examines the various **types of hard disk interface** and the way in which data flow is managed through **sector interleaving.**

Chapter 15 deals with **hard disk care and management,** and **chapter 16**, the types of **errors** to which **hard disks** are subject, and how these can be spotted by error messages from the operating system.

Viruses are responsible for some disk problems and the final chapter (**chapter 17**) deals with this important topic.

This book should be regarded as a combined reference and trouble shooter - perhaps a bit more of one than the other! This has meant that some of the material in the book has had to be duplicated to avoid too much referring back and forth for information.

More or less anything to do with computers has the habit of throwing up a great many technical terms and jargon. I have tried to reduce the jargon and technicalities to the minimum but sometimes it's unavoidable. There is a pretty comprehensive glossary - very handy when ploughing through my deathless (?deathly) prose and full of terms that will cause your friends to confer upon you the instant status of 'Computer Guru' if you're not careful.....

I have tried to make this book as error-free as possible but mistakes can sometimes occur, even in the best regulated books. Neither the author nor publisher can be held responsible for any loss or damage your files may suffer as a consequence of using this book.

Comments about specific software should be taken, unless otherwise stated, as referring to that version only, since manufacturers sometimes vary the abilities of later versions of programs.

Upper and lower case commands

DOS is not case sensitive and commands can be typed in upper or lower case letters. It is sensitive to spacing and there should always be a space between a command, and the drive letter or filename (or whatever!) to which it refers. Pressing the Enter key concludes a command line and causes the command to be executed.

This book deals only with personal computers operating under a version of DOS from Microsoft, IBM or Digital Research/Novell. It doesn't cater for those PCs running operating systems such as OS/2 or Unix.

CHAPTER 1
First aid

You have a problem with a disk...

DON'T DO ANYTHING TO THE DISK OR MACHINE JUST YET!

Before attempting to sort it out, take a little time to answer the following questions and look through the explanations. **Make a written note of your replies and other information for use during the recovery process. This will save you a lot of trouble later on:**

1. Have you used any of the following commands recently:

   FORMAT, DISKCOPY and either ERASE *.* or DEL *.* ?

If so, look at the section on **FINGER TROUBLE**

2. Have you used a data compression program such as Stacker, Superstor or Doublespace on the disk?

3. Is it your hard disk?   If YES, go to question 5

4. Is it a floppy disk?   If YES, go to question 9

5. Did your system tell you that you didn't have a hard disk when you switched it on or did you get 'Invalid drive specification' when you typed the drive letter for the hard disk?

6. Did you get any messages such as 'fixed disk error' or 'HDD controller failure'

7. Were you previously getting the occasional error message such as 'Sector not found reading drive C'?

8. Did you hear any unusual noises as the machine started up or before the possible failure (screeching, wheezing, clunking, clattering or similar)?

Now, go to question 13.

9. What size is your floppy disk (3.5" or 5.25")? Did the machine setup show that your disk drive(s) were correctly installed (360k or 1.2M for the 5.25" and 720k or 1.44M for the 3.5" types)?

10. Were you able to use the disk successfully prior to the failure?

11. Did you get error messages such as 'General failure reading drive A' or 'Sector not found reading drive B'?

12. Did you see a message such as 'FDD controller failure'?

13. Is the disk full? If so, you may be able to make space by deleting unwanted files. If it is a floppy disk, try using another formatted disk.

14. Do you have any form of backup on disk or tape? If not, how important is the data that you want to read?

15. Do you have a copy of Norton Utilities readily available?

If you do, turn to chapter 3 for further information.

Now read on...

FINGER TROUBLE

Unintentional disk formatting or erasure of files, or faulty disk copying are responsible for most disk problems, particularly if you are under pressure or feeling tired.

Typing FORMAT C: will wipe your hard disk (drive C) because most people don't think about the consequences of answering 'Y' to the 'Are you sure? Y/N' message. This is very annoying when you really wanted to format a disk in drive A, but you can sometimes recover the contents of your disk if you are using version 5 or 6 of DOS or if you have one of the utility programs such as Norton or PC Tools active in your system.

Perhaps you wanted to make a backup copy of a data disk so you typed:

```
DISKCOPY A: A:
```

(quite correctly) - but you put in the blank disk first - thus copying the formatting pattern onto the data disk. There's not a lot you can do about this except to remember in future to write protect a source disk before copying it. It's just possible that the DOS 5 UNFORMAT command will help, but only if the source disk was originally formatted under DOS 5 or 6.

Deleting or erasing files is easy. but remember that DEL *.* deletes all the files in the directory, and that most folk don't think about the 'Are you sure Y/N' message. It is fairly easy to recover these files if you don't carry out any other file maintenance before running the recovery program, and you have PC Tools or Norton Utilities available.

HARD DISKS

Hard disk failures are **most** likely to occur when the machine is first switched on, or as a result of the computer receiving a bump or jolt while switched on.

'No Hard Disk' or 'Invalid drive specification'.

Apart from early XT machines in which the various hardware options were set using switches on the motherboard, most IBM-compatible AT (286, 386 and 486) computers have a setup program, either supplied on a utility disk or as part of the BIOS (see glossary) - such as AMI, Phoenix or Award. The machines are designed to keep the information about the number and type of floppy or hard disks, the amount of memory or type of display, in a small area of memory called CMOS (or battery-backed) RAM. Sometimes this information gets corrupted or is lost because the battery runs down. In such a case, the machine will probably not start up from it's hard disk and will require the use of an internal 'Setup' program which is usually accessed by pressing one or more keys during the POST period. See the computer manual for details. Very occasionally, the system may require to be 'booted' - or started up from a floppy disk in drive A.

Likely cure:

Check if you have a hard disk in your machine, and that it is active (gentle whirring sounds). Are all the cables correctly fitted and plugged in?

Look in your computer's manual for this information - in particular, the type number for the hard disk. Sometimes you have to fill in details of the number of cylinders and heads - this information should be in your book. Check how to access the setup program and once you are in it, check EACH option to make sure it's correct and corresponds with your machine configuration. Don't start fiddling around with Advanced setup options unless you know exactly what you're up to, and how to get out of trouble if you set them incorrectly.

Check the CMOS RAM battery - the manual will tell you where it is. If you can check, it should be delivering about 3 - 4 volts. If not, it may be exhausted - either re-charge or replace.

If you don't do this, then the system will need to have all it's options set every time you switch on and this is a total pain!

Don't use the disk formatting utility in the AMI setup program if you have an IDE hard drive. In fact - don't use it at all.

This is a sure cause of 'tears before bed-time' since it carries out a very thorough low-level format of your disk, totally removing any data and a lot more besides. Unless you have access to advanced (expensive) disk re-formatting software, your IDE drive will now be as much use as a small door-stop!

Fixed disk error or HDD Controller failure

These errors mean either that the controller card has died or, more seriously, that the hard disk is not responding to the controller, usually through an internal fault.

Likely cure:

A replacement controller card of the correct type (usually from the same manufacturer although any WD-compatible controller will normally enable you to access Western Digital-compatible drives) will usually sort out the problem associated with the second message, and may also sort out the first - although this is unlikely. If there is a fixed disk error, the outlook is usually not very promising since the on-board electronics may have failed. It is sometimes possible to replace the controller board on the hard disk but usually, data recovery is beyond help, except from specialists. Some HDD controllers are part of multi-function cards and replacement can be tricky.

'Sector not found' and similar errors

This type of problem is most frequently associated with older hard cards using RLL -encoded drives, but can also happen with older MFM drives. Cylinders are very closely spaced on hard drives and the ability of the system to find information depends upon the accuracy of the information on the precise cylinder and sector locations. The read/write heads are moved across the disks by a stepper motor, one cylinder at a time, until the head is positioned over the precise cylinder as noted in the file allocation table. In most cases, there are no problems but if the drive is used in a poorly ventilated enclosure, overheating and expansion can result in mis-reading the sector information. This was a frequent source of problems in Amstrad PC1512 machines. Worn drives suffer from similar problems due to inaccurate registration of the heads on the disk surface. Once a drive shows this sort of problem, it is best to take it out of use and have it checked.

Likely cure:

Check for overheating (drives get quite warm) and see if airflow inside the case can be improved. If not, try running the machine with the lid open as a temporary measure and backup the disk as soon as possible. Very occasionally, the HDD controller card may cause problems of this sort, but this is unlikely.

Mechanical noises

Usually nasty. Not a lot you can do since the failure is either imminent or has already happened. Typically, the drive motor for the disk has seized up or the read/write heads have hit the disk platters. Some specialist firms may be able to help, but it's likely to be expensive (between ú250 and ú1000) - and not guaranteed to succeed.

A hard disk that has failed, either electronically or mechanically, is not worth attempting to salvage unless the data contained on it is very important or irreplaceable. Specialist firms quite often succeed by replacing the drive electronics board but dealing with mechanical damage is very difficult and involves dismantling the drive totally in a 'clean room' environment.

There's more information on hard disk troubles and remedies in Chapter 2.

FLOPPY DISKS

If the problem is with a floppy disk, then make a backup copy if possible.

To do this, find out which drive the floppy disk fits into (A or B) and find a formatted disk of the same size and density. Then type:

DISKCOPY d: d: (Enter)   (where 'd' is the drive letter)

Make sure that the suspect disk is write-protected and that both it and the copy disk are correctly labelled. You will be prompted to swap disks if you are copying 3.5" types, or 1.2M 5.25", since the computer does not have enough memory to copy more than 500 - 600k of files at one pass.

Put the original disk safely away and carry out any amendments on the copied disk. If you could not copy the disk, the recovery process is a lot more critical.

Size and capacity

Low capacity 5.25" (360k) are highly susceptible to magnetic fields or to being used as mats for hot drinks. High capacity 5.25" are less susceptible and 3.5" disks are fairly robust but can be affected by very strong magnets. The 5.25" types are easily damaged by being folded but 3.5" types are much tougher. AT computers allow you to specify the maximum capacity of your floppy drive(s) in the setup program and some XT disk controllers automatically recognise the type of drives connected to them. It is important to get the drive size and capacity correct, otherwise disks will be incorrectly read or formatted. Never try to format a low density disk to a higher capacity - it may work for a while but the data is unlikely to be there a few months later..... and it will serve you right for being mean - OK then, excessively cost-conscious... but disks aren't that expensive and data can be!

Likely cure:

Use 3.5" disks where possible. Check your CMOS RAM settings and remember to format the disks to the correct capacity in your drives.

Earlier use OK

Is the disk full? Did you subject it to hot coffee or a strong magnetic field or similar hazard? Even handling a 5.25" floppy with dirty fingers on the read/write slot will cause problems due to grease contamination. Did you write-protect the disk?

Likely cure:

Keep your fingers off the sensitive parts of the disk, and never drink or smoke near a computer. If the disk is full, try to make space by deleting less important files. Write protect faults are easily overcome - remove the tab on the 5.25" floppy or slide the write protect button up on 3.5" types.

'General failure', 'Sector not found' or 'Seek error' messages

The first usually occurs when an unprepared disk (unformatted) is put in a disk drive. Whilst annoying, it isn't serious since a disk can be formatted very easily. The Sector not found (or seek error) messages are more important since they indicate that a disk drive is faulty. This may occur through mechanical wear and tear or through the drive being dropped or otherwise abused. I had experienced this some years ago when I was using an old computer to format some 40 track disks for me, which were not readable by my more modern machine. There are between 48 and 135 tracks per inch on floppy disks, so head alignment is critical. I found out that one of the disk drives was out of alignment as a result of a fall.

Likely cure:

Go and format a supply of disks to the correct density. Otherwise, have the drive checked if you suspect that it is old, or has been subject to a mechanical shock (like being dropped on the floor!). It isn't usually worth repairing damaged floppy drives subject to seek errors - typically, a new drive costs ú40 - 50 and a repair will cost almost as much, if you can find a firm to do it for you.

Controller failure

This is unlikely to happen but can be a nuisance, particularly when the FDD controller is part of a multiple card (such as a printer/serial/hard disk controller). There are rarely any problems with disk format.

Likely cure;

It is possible to obtain replacement FDD controllers quite cheaply (ú15 or so) but ensure that the floppy controller function of the multiple I/O card is inactivated. This is usually done by adding or removing a link on the card. If you cannot do this, then the entire card must be replaced.

Backup available?

If you do have a backup of a recent version of what's on your disk, then you may be lucky and lose only the most recent data when you come to restore the files to your hard or floppy disk.

Before attempting to restore, take a little time to re-read the instructions which came with the backup program and/or hardware. If you backed up to an external tape streamer, then don't rely on your memory for details of the commands needed to extract files from the tape. I did, once, with unfortunate results - I lost 3 months' work on a book!

If you have no backup available, then you are in trouble. It is often possible to retrieve data from floppy disks and sometimes from hard disks when disaster strikes, but the tools available to you through DOS are fairly limited. Utility programs are much more helpful - but only if you have a copy immediately to hand.

If you cannot retrieve the data yourself, either because you do not have the time or sang-froid to carry out what may be a tricky operation, you will need to contact an expert firm. This is expensive - many such firms charge £150 - 250 for an initial consultation with no guarantee of success. Depending upon the difficulty of the problem, you may be charged £50 - 100 per hour for data recovery. Is it worth it? Even if the data can be recovered, it may be so damaged, corrupted or fragmentary as to be useless. See chapter 5 for further information.

CHAPTER 2
Disaster Strikes!

It happened!

Your hard disk has died on you!   BUT in the immortal words of Douglas Adams (Hitch-Hiker's Guide to the Galaxy) - **DON'T PANIC**

Stop a minute and think. Carefully!

Did you back up the contents recently and do you know where the disks are?

Is the rest of the system working (noises, lights and things on the screen)?

If it isn't, has some joker pulled out the power plug or switched your system off? (it can and does happen)

Has the machine shown any signs of unusual behaviour - such as sudden sluggishness, files which go missing for no good reason, or strange happenings on the screen?

If this is the case, you might have a virus in your system.   Have a look at chapter 17 for some advice on tackling the problem - which might have caused damage to your hard disk.

Do you have any of these following messages on the screen:

1. Drive X: not ready

2. Invalid drive specification

3. Non-system disk or disk error
   Replace and strike any key when ready

4. Missing operating system

5. Error loading operating system

6. Disk boot failure

7. Bad or Missing Command Interpreter

8. Cannot load COMMAND.COM, system halted

9. Invalid COMMAND.COM, system halted

10. Cannot read file allocation table

11. File allocation table bad, drive X
   Abort, Retry, Fail?

12. General failure error reading drive X
   Abort, Retry, Fail?

13. Sector not found

14. Data error

15. Write fault error / Read fault error

(The letter X means any legitimate disk drive letter from A onwards.)

What do they mean?

1. If a drive which has previously worked, gives this message, then either it or it's controller card may well have died.

2. The CMOS memory which holds the details of the computer setup may have been corrupted. You will probably need to refer to your computer's user guide for help in sorting this one out

3. Self-explanatory - the disk in the floppy drive did not have an operating system when you tried to boot from it. Take the disk out and try again either with or without a boot disk.

4. No trace of an operating system on the hard disk - possibly wiped or over-written.

5. Self explanatory

6. The hard disk didn't respond, and no disk with a operating system (such as your emergency boot disk) was in the floppy drive.

7. COMMAND.COM on the hard disk has been over-written or corrupted.

8. COMMAND.COM probably corrupted.

9. COMMAND.COM probably not the same version as the system files.

10. At some stage the first FAT has been damaged

11. Similar to the previous message but giving you a chance to do something about the problem.

12. This one is potentially very nasty if it happens with the hard disk. Try pressing R to retry the read operation. If the message persistently appears, re-boot the system, but if that doesn't help, then switch off and leave the system to cool down. The error is sometimes caused by an overheated hard disk (usually as a result of a ventilation problem), but it would be sensible to back up the disk in case the error is a forewarning of disk failure.

13. This type of error usually means that the relevant sector could not be accessed and is usually due to a faulty or damaged disk.

14. A Data Error usually means that there is a bad spot on the disk where the formatting process has failed.

15. The normal cause of this, apart from a badly inserted disk, is when a disk becomes corrupted by overheating, magnetic fields or by being physically damaged.

Errors 13 - 15 are sometimes overcome by Retrying the operation a few times, but any disk which causes these messages to occur should be treated with suspicion, and if it proves possible to recover data from it, the disk should then be disposed of. Floppy disks with such problems are not worth keeping and hard disks should be subjected to detailed investigation with a utility program such as Norton Disc Doctor or Disk Technician Gold before being used for any critical purpose.

What if there are NO messages on screen?

Try the following:

* **Is the monitor plugged in and switched on, and the video-lead properly installed in the video card. (A very common problem, not confined to novices either). Did you adjust the controls on the monitor?**

* Did you switch off, then switch on again a few seconds later? If so, the power supply may have objected and 'locked up'. Switch off, leave for a minute or two and then switch on again. (Another common fault, of which I've been guilty from time to time!).

If these don't fix your problem, then you will have to carry out a well-defined series of procedures to sort out the problem or, failing that, to help you get to the root of the problem.

1. Turn the system off and then, after half a minute, turn it on again. This frequently works! Don't ask me why, but it does....

If you have something on the screen -

2. Press CTRL+ALT+DEL to re-boot the system. Get into the CMOS setup by pressing the relevant keys (for example, <DEL> if you have a AMI BIOS - see your computer's user guide for other BIOS information).

Check that the entries for video and hard and floppy drives are correct and amend if necessary.

3. Take out any disk in drive A and re-boot with CTRL+ALT+DEL.

If this doesn't get your system going, drive C is sick or dead!

4. Put the write-protected boot disk in drive A, making sure that the disk in place and the retaining latch is closed. Press CTRL+ALT+DEL to re-boot the system.

If this works, your system will boot up. Once it has booted, delete the old, defective copy of COMMAND by copying COMMAND.COM from the floppy.

```
COPY command.com c:\dos\command.com
```

should do it. If not, and the system says that you cannot copy COMMAND.COM, see if you can read the directory on drive C with the DIR command.

5. DIR. If this produced an error message, your hard disk is really damaged - otherwise if you didn't get an error message and no files were listed, you have either an unused hard disk (unusual) or a disk from which all files have been erased.

6. Try the UNDELETE command if you've used DOS 5 or 6. This could be a life-saver.

7. Assuming that the hard disk is working but shows no files in it's directory, another user or yourself might have accidentally formatted it. Whoops! The UNFORMAT command on the boot disk will sort this one out if you type :

unformat c: (or whatever the drive letter is!)

The process is pretty easy to carry out.

8. If the wipe-out was not accidental, you could have caught a VIRUS or have been the subject of a bit of sabotage. It is worth trying to put back the system files on the disk so, with your boot disk in place, type:

```
SYS C:
```

When the files have been copied, you will get a message on the screen to say that the system has been transferred. Take out the boot disk and press CTRL/ALT/DEL to boot the system from the hard disk. If you are fortunate, your system will re-start, but you will have to restore all of your files from backups.

If this doesn't work, your disk's logical structure may have been damaged.

9. If you cannot start your system by using the procedure in point 8, the only alternative is to carry out a high level re-format, in order to sort out damage to the disk's logical structure. Boot up with the floppy disk, and type the following command:

```
FORMAT C: /S /V
```

This will format the hard disk, transfer the system files and prompt you for a disk volume label.

If this was achieved without any problems, you can begin to restore files from your backups.

10. There is a remote possibility that whatever wiped the files may also have deleted partition information on the disk. In this case, you will need to run the FDISK program on your boot disk by typing:

```
FDISK
```

and when you have answered the questions, the disk will be correctly set up to take a format as in step 9.

11. If your disk will not respond to re-formatting, or you experience further problems once it has been re-formatted, you have two choices.

(a) Get hold of a copy of Norton Utilities or PC Tools and use either the Disk Doctor or Disk Fix program - or

(b) Count your pennies and find a professional repair shop that will do the job for you.

I hope that it didn't come to step 11

Battery problems and the CMOS RAM

One problem that sometimes occurs, particularly with older PCs, is the failure of the battery which keeps the CMOS RAM information intact. This is usually either a small, rechargeable NiCad type (about 3.6 or 4.8 volts) which is trickle-charged when the machine is switched on, or a lithium dry (non-rechargeable) battery. If the computer has a rechargeable battery, and hasn't been used for several months, the rechargeable battery will have run down and the CMOS information lost. Leave such a system switched on for several hours to recharge.

Lithium batteries normally last 3 - 5 years and, once exhausted, must be replaced.

This particular problem is most easily diagnosed because once you have re-programmed the CMOS memory, and switched off after your work, the next time you switch on the system, the information will have been lost, yet again!

Restoring your backup files

Your backup files will probably be on floppy disks or on tape. Do take a moment to remember what program you used to carry out the backup and look in the operating manual or instruction booklet for the correct form of the command you have to use.

This is very important otherwise you may well end up by backing up files to the wrong drive or worse still, deleting them.

Restoring from tapes usually makes use of software provided by the tape streamer manufacturer, although some people like to use the tape backup and restore facility in PC Tools.

The majority of backups are done using the DOS BACKUP program and the files can be restored by using the RESTORE program which is also available in DOS.

The disks containing the backups are read, usually in drive A and restored to whichever drive you want, so that:

```
RESTORE A: D: /S
```

will restore all files from a compressed form on drive A to an uncompressed form on drive D. The /S switch ensures that files are restored to the correct directory on the destination drive. The process is automatic and you are prompted to insert new disks as required until the backup is complete.

It is possible to backup single files, or the contents of a single directory, and there are additional switches which can be very useful - so that /M restores only those files which were wiped or modified since the last backup, and /N restores all those files which are currently not on the destination disk. This is a pretty useful switch, and all the switches can be used in combination so that:

```
RESTORE A: D: /S /N
```

restores all subdirectories and puts any new files not currently on the hard disk.

CHAPTER 3
Coping and Recovering if you have Norton Utilities

A. IF IT'S YOUR HARD DISK (go to B if it's definitely a floppy disk)

Some important advice -

"If you have an emergency situation and you've purchased the Norton Utilities to restore your hard disk or recover deleted files, **do not install the Norton Utilities on your hard disk.** Any new files copied to the hard disk might overwrite erased files, preventing a complete recovery".

(from the Norton Utilities emergency procedure)

Borrow or buy a copy of Norton Utilities if you don't already have it.

Check the Manual for the version of Norton which you are using for the disk numbers which contain the following programs: UNFORMAT, UNERASE and NDD. Make a note because the disk numbers vary according to the disk size.

Unformatting your hard disk after an accidental format:

1. If your hard disk was accidentally formatted after a hard day's number-crunching, start your computer using a floppy boot disk with the same version of DOS which was originally used to format the disk.

2. Replace the DOS disk in drive A with the NU disk containing the UNFORMAT program. Type a:UNFORMAT and press Enter. Follow the instructions on-screen and select the drive to Unformat.

3. Press the Enter key to start the unformatting. The program automatically guides you through the process.

4. At the end, quit NU and re-boot the system from the hard disk. All should be well.

Recovering erased files

1. At the prompt (C>), insert the correct NU disk in drive A. Type a:UNERASE and press the Enter key. The Unerase program starts and allows you to select the file or directory to be unerased.

2. Select the file to be unerased (if you cannot see it, press F10 which activates a series of Pull-Down menus - from which you should select the option to 'view all directories' from the file menu).

3. Highlight the file to be unerased, select the unerase button.

4. Type in the first letter of the name of the file (any letter will do since DOS deletes files by changing the first letter of the file name to a ?); UNERASE will automatically recover the file for you and the replacement first letter can be altered later if you want.

Diagnosing a sick disk with Disk Doctor

If the hard disk is non-functional, boot up the machine with a DOS disk and insert the Norton Utilities disk with the NDD program into drive A.

If the hard disk IS working, simply insert the disk with the NDD program in drive A. 1. Type a:NDD and press the Enter key.

2. From the Menu, select Diagnose Disk

3. Remove the Norton disk from drive A and, if necessary, insert the defective floppy disk in the appropriate drive.

4. Select the drive to diagnose and press the Enter key.

5. NDD carries out most of its operations automatically and should cope with the majority of problems you might have encountered.

B. IT'S A FLOPPY FAILURE

The first thing to do is to try to make a backup copy of the floppy disk using DISKCOPY. Never do nasty things like data recovery on the original disk!!!

1. Log into the DOS directory on the hard disk. Write protect the defective disk (sticky label or slide). Find a disk of identical size and capacity and make sure that it doesn't contain any important information, and is not write-protected. Label it as 'Damaged disk backup'.

2. Type DISKCOPY a: a: (or b: b:, depending upon which disk drive is required) and press the Enter key. Insert the damaged disk, and follow the instructions regarding disk swapping as required.

3. Make sure that the original disk is properly labelled and put away safely. Carry out all further operations on the copy. (This will be identical to the original disk because DISKCOPY gives an exact replica, including all the faults except those which were caused by a physical problem on the original disk!

4. Take the copy disk out, and decide which emergency treatment it needs - unformatting or, more often file recovery or disk doctoring. Insert the relevant Norton Utilities disk as detailed above, and call up the appropriate program.

5. Insert the copy disk and proceed as directed.

Good luck!

CHAPTER 4
Using DOS utilities to recover lost data

Until the advent of DOS version 5.0 and DR-DOS 6.0, the range of file management and data recovery programs available as part of the DOS package were pretty rudimentary and their effects are sometimes drastic and unhelpful.

These programs include CHKDSK, COPY, DEBUG (MSDOS) or SID (DRDOS), with RECOVER, and their modes of action are fairly unsophisticated when compared with modern utility programs such as the latest versions of the Norton Utilities or PC Tools.

CHKDSK can be used to repair damaged file structures, COPY can be used both to transfer unaffected files from a damaged disk to a fresh destination as well as for recovering file allocation table damage (FAT). It is possible to use the editing facilities within DEBUG or SID to repair small amounts of damage to files and RECOVER, as it's name suggests, does offer some chance of file recovery.

The advent of DRDOS 6.0 and MSDOS 5.0 in 1991 added several important tools to the recovery and file management armoury. These include two utilities for reversing the effects of accidental file deletion or disk formatting (UNDELETE and UNFORMAT) and MIRROR (MSDOS) or DISKMAP (DRDOS) which track the changes made to the file allocation table (FAT) as files are added to or deleted from the disk. This information is used by the UNDELETE and UNFORMAT commands to recover the disk contents or files.

In this chapter, the DOS commands (for the Microsoft/IBM and Digital Research versions) and their use in data recovery are examined. If your problem can be sorted out using a DOS utility, it could save you the cost of purchasing the commercial packages, but at the risk of spending a considerable amount of time (and temper) achieving the desired recovery.

CHKDSK

This is a powerful and quite versatile command. It is usually employed to report on the disk space availability of a drive and the DOS memory allocation but it can also report upon the state of files on the disk and any fragmentation, and can even carry out limited repairs.

Major functions

Directory and FAT inspection for discrepancies, particularly fragmented files and 'lost clusters' (parts of files which appear to have lost their parent file).

Usage

```
CHKDSK [d:] [pathname][filename] [/F] [/V]
```

Square brackets indicate optional parameters or switches

d: is the drive letter to be examined pathname and filename specify files to be checked

/F allows corrections to be written to the disk if errors are found.

/V displays file names as processed If the /F parameter is not included, any correction of discrepancies are not written to disk.

When to use CHKDSK

CHKDSK compares the FAT with the directory and subdirectory and will adjust the disk directory so that it is in agreement with the FAT. For this reason, it should be run without the /F parameter so that the extent of any problem can be judged. Quite often, the directory structure is correct and either or both of the file allocation tables may be damaged. The use of /F overwrites the directory structure and repair of the FAT is less easy. If you are sure, run CHKDSK with the /F parameter, and it will convert lost clusters and chains of clusters (referred to as allocation units) into files with the name FILENNNN.CHK (where N is a digit from 0 - 9).

This effectively legalises the errant data and allows you to look at it using one of the viewing utilities.

Problems of this nature are fairly minor and usually result from a failure to exit a program correctly - if, for example, the program appears to hang the computer and you resort to the reset button or Ctrl-Alt-Del sequence to re-boot the machine. Some programs make a lot of use of temporary files and buffers and normal program exits allow the system to remove this garbage before leaving the application. The re-boot sequence does not enable DOS to update the directory entry for the file and the details of the directory entry may not match the true state of the file.

When a file is newly written to a disk, the DOS allocates space for that file in the FAT. If the file is modified, additional clusters are allocated in the FAT and a chain of clusters results. If the system is closed down abnormally, before DOS can close the file, any additional material may not be correctly allocated to space on the disk and thus becomes a series of lost clusters.

Lost clusters are units of data storage with a marker indicating that they are in use, but no corresponding claim to a directory entry. In this case, the clusters are a fragment of a file which could possibly be recovered. If you answer 'N' to the 'Convert lost chains to files' dialogue, DOS frees the space that would have been in use and other files can use it. Answering 'Y' leads to the formation of FILENNNN.CHK files. On examination, these may be found to contain recognisable fragments of text but mostly they will be unintelligible.

COPY

This command enables you to transfer data from one disk to another, and can be thought of as a very simple data recovery command.

Usage

COPY is fairly straightforward in use but has an awkward feature called file concatenation (joining) which enables the contents of several files to be copied into another.

```
COPY [d:][sourcepathname]filename [/A][/B]
     [d:][dest.pathname][filename] [/A][/B][/V]
```

Square brackets indicate optional parameters or switches

d: is the drive letter to be examined pathname and filename specify source and destination files
/A treats the file as an ASCII text file
/B treats the file as a binary format file
/V verifies that the data as copied is accurate.

The /A parameter copies all text up to but excluding the EOF (end of file) mark (Ctrl-Z) with a source file but adds the EOF marker to the end of a destination file.

The /B parameter copies the entire file, including any EOF marks wherever they occur. It does NOT add the EOF marker to destination files.

COPY defaults to the /B parameter

DOS has a number of ways of deciding when it gets to the end of a file. At that point, it terminates processing of the file and if this DOS-determined ending is not the same as the real end of the file, you have a problem. One or more of the three following conditions determine when an end of file is reached:

a. DOS encounters a FAT end of chain marker

b. The total number of bytes read by DOS is the same as the number in the directory listing

c. Rarely, (and only with the /A parameter in operation) the presence of an EOF marker (Ctrl-Z or 1A {in hexadecimal}) in an ASCII file.

Problems arise when files contain characters which DOS interprets as an EOF or end of chain (EOC) markers which occur before the true end of the file. These may arise through faulty copying or data corruption. Disagreements between the file length as shown in the directory and the allowable file length as recorded in the FAT may also occur as a result of data corruption or improper program exits (as previously discussed under CHKDSK). The individual cluster size on, for example, a 720K floppy disk is 1024 bytes (1 Kilobyte or 2 sectors of 512 bytes).

Files are allocated to clusters and if a small file spans less than 2 clusters, the EOF character is followed by a lot of padding characters to fill up the space. Longer files will occupy more sectors but always, the space between the end of file marker and the next sector boundary is padded.

There is no restriction on the type of disk that can be used as the destination, apart from the fact that it should be correctly formatted. In data recovery, the destination disk is usually a floppy disk. The COPY command is particularly useful if you are using the RECOVER command and a single file is involved.

DEBUG and SID

DEBUG is the MSDOS version and SID, the DRDOS version of program debugging tools which are used by programmers in the development of assembly language programs.

Major functions

Their main use is for making minor adjustments to programs (hence the term, debugging' or for directly altering the contents of a disk sector - the typical use in data recovery.

These programs are able to display or enter data to or from any location in memory, read or write disk sectors into or from memory. They can also be used for writing short assembly language programs or for examining and modifying sections of files which may be faulty.

Using either DEBUG or SID for data recovery is most unwise unless you have some prior experience with the programs. Microsoft and Digital Research provide some information in their DOS user manuals.

To start DEBUG, (which should be in your DOS path), simply type:

```
DEBUG [d:] [pathname] [filename] [arguments]
```

Square brackets indicate optional parameters or switches

d: is the drive letter to be examined
pathname and **filename** specify the path to the source file which is to be debugged.
arguments refers to various parameters and
switches which can be used by DEBUG

When DEBUG is active, it uses a hyphen as it's command prompt (quite unlike the C> prompt used by DOS. Exit DEBUG by typing Q.

SID is started in a similar manner

```
SID [d:][pathname][filename]
```

Square brackets indicate optional parameters or switches

d: is the drive letter to be examined
pathname and **filename** specify the path to the source file which
is to   be debugged.

The command prompt is a hash '#' symbol and the parameters for SID's
operation are entered at the command prompt.   Quitting the program is
done by typing Q or Ctrl+C.

RECOVER

This is a very powerful utility which regains readable information from
a bad or defective disk.

Major functions

The program reads a file sector by sector and recovers data from the
good (readable) sectors; unreadable data is lost but all recovered data is
written to the root directory. The file allocation table is marked so that
the bad sectors are not used again.

The program is HIGHLY DANGEROUS.   Don't use it unless you
understand what it can do, since casual use may well render your disk
totally unreadable.   You have been warned!

RECOVER can operate on single files or the whole disk - the latter is
the option to avoid unless the disk's directory is unusable.

```
RECOVER [d:][pathname]filename
```

Square brackets indicate optional parameters or switches

d: is the drive letter to be examined
pathname and **filename** specify the path to the source file which is to be recovered.

To operate on the whole disk, type:

```
RECOVER d:
```

Recovered files are named as FILENNNN.REC (where N is a digit from 0 - 9). They do not have their original names. Microsoft recommend that files are recovered one at a time and you must know the name of the file that you are trying to recover. Lost data will have to be re-entered - possibly using a debugger.

Data can be preserved by using a combination of the COPY and RECOVER commands - for example, if a file load is interrupted by a message such as:

```
Sector not found error reading drive B
Abort, Retry, Ignore, Fail?
```

The natural reaction is to Retry the load - you may have to do this several times before the file actually loads fully. In this case, save the file under a different name, or on another drive. If several retry attempts don't work, it is best to Abort the load.

It may be possible to overcome the problem if the file is ASCII text. Make a copy of the dodgy file using the COPY command with a slightly different name - for example;

```
COPY TEXT.DOC TEXTNEW.DOC
```

The copy process will work until the Sector not found error occurs - but now you press I to Ignore the problem. In this case, the bad sector(s) are ignored and the process can complete a file transfer in full. The TEXTNEW.DOC file will be faulty but intact on either side of the bad sectors.

It is normally necessary to edit the recovered file to remove the gibberish, but at least the rest of the file is safe.

Program and other binary files are not economically recoverable by this process.

The next stage is to use RECOVER to mark the offending sectors as bad in the FAT by typing:

RECOVER filename (in this case, TEXT.DOC)

RECOVER reports the number of bytes recovered out of the total and the old file is still on disk, but truncated at the beginning of the bad sector. The bad sector is marked in the FAT and you should then delete the old file. CHKDSK will show how many bad sectors exist.

File recovery by this route will almost certainly be time consuming and is unlikely to be reliable. Frankly, I would not recommend it. Far better to upgrade at least to DOS 5 and save yourself a lot of trouble.

CHAPTER 5
Getting organised for survival......

Most PC users are pretty casual about survival - they use their favourite machine (or the machine they love to hate) day after day with never a thought about the consequences of a disk disaster.

When their disk dies, they haven't a clue about what to do - and they will probably end up by panicking or losing their temper.

Moments of panic or anger are not the best times to try and salvage valuable data and you may well lose the lot if you're not careful.

But, as far as you are concerned, survival is pretty important (otherwise you wouldn't have bought this book!) - and you'll make sure that you are as well-prepared as possible for that stomach-churning moment - if it happens!

It's worth remembering that if the hard disk dies on you for an electrical or mechanical reason, data recovery could be either difficult or expensive - or both. The best protection is a regular backup.

Cheap and cheerful?

The minimum you can get away with, and have a reasonably hassle-free chance of sorting out the commoner problems such as deleting all the file on a disk or formatting it, is to install MSDOS 5.0 on your system.

This because DOS 5 contains a utility program called MIRROR. Load this program when your system starts up and it will keep track of all the files which you delete, and maintain a copy of your hard disk's contents. If you have an accidental format, or delete everything on a disk, the data collected by MIRROR will be used by the UNDELETE and UNFORMAT programs and your disk's structure will be restored.

This has saved many users' sanity!

The MIRROR command is added to your AUTOEXEC.BAT file as follows:

```
MIRROR c: /TC
```

which loads delete tracking for drive C. If you have a drive D as well, the following command will load MIRROR with delete tracking for drives C and D:

```
MIRROR c: d: /TC /TD
```

This sort of precaution will deal with most disk disasters, excepting those which arise because the hard disk has 'died' mechanically or electronically.

In common with other DOS versions, DOS 5 has a backup facility which, if used sensibly and regularly, will make sure that you suffer minimum inconvenience if a disk does crash or become unreadable. You can backup part or all of your disks, including subdirectories and it is possible to backup just those files which are new, or modified since the last backup was carried out. Just remember - backup regularly - weekly or even on a daily basic. Keep the backup disks safely, and remember to keep all your other disks safe as well. This means that they should be kept clear of magnetic fields such as television sets or loudspeakers, and kept at a reasonable room temperature - too hot, and the data may become unreliable.

DOS 6 has a few additional features compared with DOS 5 including an anti-virus program and an enhanced version of UNDELETE with various levels of deletion tracking and a disk de-fragmenter. I must admit to being less enthusiastic about this version.

Apart from installing DOS 5 or a more recent version on your hard disk, you should always make a couple of emergency boot disks. If you are critically dependent upon your software applications, you should always make copies of the original disks by using the DISKCOPY program.

```
DISKCOPY A: A:
```

Allows you to copy the contents of a disk onto one of the same capacity in drive A.   Replace the A with a B if you need to use the other drive. The program prompts you to change from the source disk to a destination disk and vice-versa from time to time since the computer hasn't got enough memory to store all of the disk's information at once. When the process is complete, don't forget to label the disk straight away.   You cannot use the DISKCOPY program to copy low capacity disks to high capacity (or vice-versa) neither will it allow copying between different sizes of disk.

Making an emergency boot disk is quite straightforward.   Put a new disk in drive A, and type the following:

```
FORMAT A: /S /V
```

This prepares the disk, adds an operating system and asks for a label name. It's a good idea to make 2 copies - the following files are needed for proper operation in case of emergency: CHKDSK.EXE, FDISK.EXE, FORMAT.COM, RESTORE.EXE, SYS.COM, UNDELETE.EXE and UNFORMAT.COM. The formatting process will also have included the hidden system files and COMMAND.COM; the remaining files should be in your DOS directory.   Suppose it was on drive C: - the command would be:

```
COPY C:\DOS\CHKDSK.EXE A:   (or FDISK.EXE etc.)
```

Copy your AUTOEXEC.BAT and CONFIG.SYS files from your hard disk on to one of the disks, together with any special programs (like for example, any fancy disk capacity doubling software or video/disk/printer drivers).   Set the write-protection tab or sticker to prevent any further changes and label the disks as 'simple boot' and 'emergency boot' respectively. Put them away safely, just in case you need them. The emergency boot disk is the most important but the other disk will be most handy if you have to carry out detailed system testing.

A digression on filenames

Many PC users aren't very well acquainted with the way in which DOS deals with files. A little revision may be useful, particularly if you need to back up or restore your programs and data.

Remember that a DOS filename has two parts - the filename (up to 8 characters) and the extension (up to 3 characters); the two parts of the name are separated by a full stop. This chapter is filed on my computer as SURVIVAL.DOC - the filename is SURVIVAL and the extension is DOC. Some files may not have an extension - it's optional.

If you are copying files or doing things in directories, you can use the * character to represent a group of from 1 to 8 characters or the ? character to represent any single one of a range of characters. So, *.DOC would represent all the DOC files on a drive, whereas for example, ?ETTER.TXT could mean either BETTER.TXT, LETTER.TXT or even úETTER.TXT or any other legal combination of symbols and letters. The ? character can be used anywhere in the filename so, for example LETTER?.TXT could represent a range of files, for example LETTER0.TXT through to LETTER9.TXT or even LETTERA.TXT to LETTERZ.TXT.

Right - you now know enough about files to do a good job of backing up the files you've got on your hard disk.

Backup your hard disk?

Sounds like a good idea, so why do so many computer users forget to do it?

There are a number of commercial and shareware programs that will backup your files, as well as the BACKUP command in DOS. You can backup on floppy disks (the usual methods) or use a tape streamer which will probably do the job faster.

Since BACKUP comes as part of your DOS, why not try it? A single command will enable you to back up an entire hard disk onto a series of disks as a series of compressed format files (this saves space and reduces the number of floppies you need). Files saved by the BACKUP command must be decompressed by means of the RESTORE command (also part of DOS).

Using BACKUP

There are three ways in which files on a disk can be backed up - all of them, some of them or only those files which have been changed, or are new since your last backup. The last type of operation is called an incremental backup.

To back up all of the files on hard disk C onto floppy disks in your A drive, type the following:

```
BACKUP C: A: /S
```

This backs up all of the files on drive C, including the subdirectories and associated files. It's not wise to leave out the /S switch

A partial or selective back up can be carried out if you just want to keep certain files - such as all files with a particular name. To do this for all your .LET files on in the main (or root) directory of drive D, just type:

```
BACKUP D:\*.LET B:
```

Which transfers all .LET files to drive B; adding the /S switch extends the command to backup all .LET files on the disk.

An incremental backup is extremely useful if you only want to backup files which are new or have been modified since your last backup. It saves on time and disks, naturally, and is selected by adding the /M switch to the command:

BACKUP D: A: /S /M So this will backup only those files on the whole of disk drive D which have been modified since the previous backup. In addition, it will backup all new files opened since that time.

To be really well-organised, it is good practice to get the system to produce a backup log. This is a file which contains information about all the files which have been backed up in the current operation. The log file switch (/L) can be added to any of the above command lines and causes BACKUP to generate a file (excitingly-named BACKUP.LOG) in the root directory of the hard drive. The log file is a very useful piece of information and it's good practice to print it out and keep it with the backup disks.

```
TYPE D:BACKUP.LOG>PRN
```

This will, if your printer is attached to your PC and ready to print, produce a copy of the log file.

Be Prepared

It's very wise, before trouble strikes, to find out about your computer system. Have a folder in which you can keep the following information:

Type number of processor (e.g. 80386sx)

How much memory is fitted (megabytes)

What BIOS is fitted (e.g. Award, AMI)

How do you get into the BIOS to alter it's configuration

(press the DEL, F1 or whatever combination of keys)

Is there an option for Advanced SETUP?

How do you get into it?

What size of hard disk (megabytes)

What type number (usually between 1 and 47 in the setup program)

How many cylinders and heads does it have

Has it been prepared with Disk Manager or a similar program

Has it been 'compressed' by Stacker, Superstor or Doublespace

What capacity are your disk drive(s) (360K or 1.2 M for 5.25" and 720K or 1.44 M for 3.5")

What type of video adapter are you using (monochrome, CGA, EGA or VGA)?

Write down what version of DOS you're using and any particular features of the system such as compressed drives (note the version number of the compression software if it isn't DOS 6 Doublespace).

Some of this information will be readily accessible through the manuals provided with the machine, but you may have to get some from the machine itself, via it's built-in setup program.

This information is held in a small area of separate battery-powered memory called the CMOS setup, and retained, even when the machine is switched off. It's purpose is to inform the machine about itself and its components when it is first switched on.

If you need to access the setup program in your computer, you need to press one or more keys during the boot-up sequence. The precise key(s) needed will depend upon the BIOS (basic input/output system)

fitted. The commonest types of BIOS fitted are those from AMI or Award, and you can usually tell which one you have by looking at the first few lines which appear on the screen after you switch it on.

The AMI BIOS can be accessed by pressing the <DEL> key during the boot-up, and the Award BIOS by holding down the CTRL key and pressing the ALT and ESC keys at the same time. It is possible to alter the details in the BIOS either by typing in numbers or by using the cursor keys or page up/down keys. Don't touch any key until you have made a note of the current settings. Even then, check carefully to see which key(s) you need to press to alter values or to exit from the setup BEFORE you do anything else.

The golden rule is - don't touch it if it's correct!

If it isn't - and you'd be surprised about the number of machines whose BIOS settings are wrong, then setting up the correct number and capacity of disk drives is easy. The setting for the hard disk is probably correct, and should only be changed if you have incontrovertible proof that it has been incorrectly set up. Don't take the machine apart to find out unless it is yours, out of guarantee and you know how to put it together again! The reason for the use of type numbers stems from the early days of IBM PC-ATs. Hard disks could be purchased from a number of manufacturers, so instead of specifying a particular model - e.g. a Seagate ST225 or a Rodime 204, a type number was used for each combination of capacity, cylinders and heads. The original system had 15 type numbers, but AMI, Award and Phoenix BIOSes have extended this to 47 or more as the capacity of hard disks has increased.

N.B. Life is never simple and the type numbers, particularly those beyond 15 are not necessarily compatible between BIOSes.

Other desirable utilities

If you exchange disks with other users, there is a chance that you will at some time, pick up a virus. DOS 6 has an anti-virus program which is pretty good and is based on a utility from Central Point who produce PC Tools, but if you're using other DOS versions, you should consider a package such as McAfee anti-virus utilities (which is shareware) or, if you have rather more money, Dr Solomon's Toolkit, which is very comprehensive and excellent. I would not like to be without my copy of Norton Utilities - which represents excellent value. It currently has the edge on PC Tools in an emergency situation since you can actually use several important utilities direct from the installation disks, without actually installing it. PC Tools is an excellent program once it's installed, but in the nature of human behaviour, 'you bought it last week and hadn't got around to installing it when your disk gave up on you'. PC Tools directs you to make a recovery disk with all sorts of useful programs on it which will enable you to sort out a damaged disk in the same way as Norton. Version 7 of Norton is the only currently available utility which will deal properly with compressed disk partitions.

Recent versions of both these programs are available for quite modest prices, but for shiny, up to date versions, you're looking at ú80 - 100. DOS 6 isn't all that cheap after the initial launch discounting, and unless you want to use the disk capacity doubling or the memory management, I don't think that it's really worth it if you can get hold of DOS 5.0.

What now?

You've taken note of the advice I've given here and you've bought or acquired some software.

Read the installation instructions before you start. When it's all there, READ THE INSTRUCTION MANUALS CAREFULLY. This is to ensure that you:

(a) remember what software you've got on the disk and,

(b) have some sort of idea how to use it!

Then read through them again! Put them somewhere where you can find them in a hurry (so that means you can't use one to prop up your computer desk.....)

If you encounter problems, try to sort these out with the firm from whom you purchased the hardware or software as soon as they show up . It's a good idea to find out if the firm has a help-line which you can contact - if only for a limited time after your purchase, before you place the order. They should be able to give assistance since they are supposed to be familiar with the product. Not every firm can do this, and if you are likely to need a lot of after-sales support, don't expect to get it from non-specialist retailers whose prices are often very keen. They probably won't have the profit margin which would allow them to employ a helpline person.

USEFUL ADDRESSES

Where can I get reliable advice on books, or get hold of information or low cost software?

Who fixes dead disks? How much will it cost me?

Shareware and other programs:

Try the following who supply a wide range of PD and Shareware:

PC Star, PO Box 164, Cardiff CF5 4SF.

PC Independent Users' Group, 87 High Street, Tonbridge, Kent TN9 1RX.

Shareware Marketing, 3a Queen Street, Seaton, Devon, EX12 2NY.

Public Domain and Shareware Library, Winscombe House, Crowborough, Sussex, TN6 1UL

There are lots of other firms - find them in the computer magazines. Most are reliable but there are quite considerable differences in prices between firms. PCIUG give discounts for members and PC-Star has some very good deals.

Biological Software, 23 Darwin Close, Orpington, Kent BR6 7EP supplies specialised compilations of shareware and PD utilities for PCs. These are particularly intended for disk management, data recovery as well as system testing and setup. Ask for details - an SAE is appreciated.

Books:

If you want a book on a particular topic - and you're not sure what to buy, contact the following for impartial advice:

Just Computer Books, 111 Court Road, Malvern, Worcs. WR14 3EF. (0684 568095)

They are able to get just about any computer book in print pretty rapidly, and specialise in mail order. There's a charge for postage, of course.

Helplines:

If you need help with your computer at any time, it's worth considering a subscription to PCIUG (address as above or phone them at 0732 771512). The Group has a good Helpline and membership is available both to individuals and companies. If you're not an expert, then this would be a shrewd move.

Data Recovery Services

Several firms offer such services - luckily, I haven't had to use them so far, but here's a couple who advertise quite widely.

Dr Allan Solomon's Data Recovery Service (S & S International, Berkley Court, Mill Street, Berkhampstead, Herts HP4 2HB) offers a 'no-fix no fee' service and can be contacted on 0800 581263 - they give a diagnosis of the problem within 4 hours and your data back within 48 hours if it is recoverable.   I've not used this firm, but I understand that they are reliable, if you're really in trouble - but their expert services won't be cheap.   If you are calling from outside the UK, +44 442 877877 will reach them.

Ontrack Data Recovery, who are contactable on 0800 243996 (+44 81 974 5522 outside the UK). Ontrack are based in Kingston upon Thames, Surrey and are part of the American company which produces Disk Manager - a well-known disk utility.   They advertise their advanced facilities and fast turn-round and are worth bearing in mind. A 'no-fix no fee' service is not specifically advertised so you should check what their policy is before committing yourself to a potentially heavy expense.

CHAPTER 6
A brief warning about elderly DOSes

Have you ever checked your DOS version number?

Does your livelihood, or that of others who work for/with you, depend upon a single PC?

If your computer is more than a couple of years old, it is probably running DOS 4 or an earlier version. Data recovery under these circumstances can be quite difficult when things go wrong.

To find out which version you have, just type VER and press the Enter key.

If the version number that's on the screen is lower than 5, you should seriously think about an upgrade. Both DOS and DRDOS in versions 5 or 6 have utility programs that can often reduce the hassle caused by a disk disaster. Upgrades cost money but disk disasters can be crippling in terms of time, money or both!

Think about it! If money is tight, try shopping around for a good price on DOS 5 - which is currently available for about £25, compared with £55 - 80 for DOS 6 (Summer 1993).

If you have a modern version of DOS but are naturally cautious and want the best chance of recovering from disk disasters, you should consider buying either Norton Utilities or PC-Tools.

Other recovery tools are available but these two packages are particularly good, and are readily available at a reasonable price. Go for version 6.01 or greater for Norton or version 7 or greater for PC-Tools. The current versions (7 and 8, respectively) are available for about £80 - £90 while some firms may have copies of the older versions on sale at bargain prices. There are some good shareware utilities if your budget is tight but they probably won't be as fully featured unless you pay a registration fee.

If your DOS version number is 4 or lower, and you're a natural Luddite who doesn't want to upgrade to these new-fangled DOSes, then you really should get hold of a copy of Norton or PC-Tools. That is, unless you really enjoy the trauma of using DEBUG, EDLIN and RECOVER and have several hours/days/weeks to spend, with no guarantee of getting back what you've lost.

CHAPTER 7
Backing-up

This is one of the easiest ways to avoid major problems if your hard disk or even an important floppy disk should prove to be unreadable at some future time.

There are several ways in which you can carry this out, and you could use either floppy disks or, if you have one, a tape streamer which uses a data cartridge (a specialised type of tape cassette).

How often?

It all depends upon the nature of the work you are doing on your PC.

A busy office should have a regular daily backup (and more frequently if the data is sensitive, irreplaceable or commercially valuable). The number of sets of backup kept should reflect the use of the system - and in a case such as this, each daily backup should be kept for 2 - 4 weeks before being discarded and the disk recycled. This could mean buying in a lot of disks, so the present trend would be to use a tape streamer which could put the whole of the contents of a pretty large hard disk onto a single tape.

The average office should backup twice a week at least, and a typical home user, about once every 2 - 4 weeks or so - but make it regular!

I try to remember to back my whole system up about once a month - and - yes, I do forget... sometimes!

Backup disks or tapes should be clearly marked with the subject matter, date and, most importantly, the date from which they can be recycled. In an office environment, the make and serial number of the machine should also be noted.

The most secure way to maintain a backup is to use your backup disk or tape sets in a sensibly sequential manner. I use 3 sets and they are recycled strictly in order over a 3 month period.

How to backup

Most of the backup software available allows you to carry out a backup of all the files on a disk or of a select number, chosen either by the user or on an incremental basis. Incremental backups take the most recent version of a file and only replace it if a more recent version exists.

Straightforward disk backups are best carried out using the improved BACKUP command in DOS 5 or 6. Restoration is also simple and involves the use of the RESTORE command. If you come across a problem, then the Online Help screens will soon prove their worth.

If you just want to backup a few files, then COPY or XCOPY will do the job for you quite adequately. Backing up a floppy disk in it's entirety is best done using DISKCOPY. I often use a file manager called XTREE GOLD which is very handy for selective backups. It's very easy to use, and allows you, amongst other things, to tag, sort and look at files and to transfer between drives. If you run out of formatted disks, then you can format your choice whilst still in XTREE - which is excellent news for the disorganised. It will prompt you to insert a new disk when the old backup disk is full. I can create backups which are compressed (ZIPped) or as archived and compressed programs which can be expanded as an when required. Not, perhaps as sophisticated as some backup programs, but heaps better than using DOS commands.

There are loads of programs which claim to carry out disk backups better than any predecessor. The best is shareware and is known as Flexiback Plus - it's excellent and is available from all good shareware sources. The current version (Summer 1993) is 2.52 and, if you like it, the author would like a ú44 registration fee.

Backing up onto floppy disks

The Five Golden Rules of Floppy disk backup

1. Backup often!

2. Backup your files onto the highest capacity disks your system can use. Make sure that they are already formatted and have a blank label that can be written on with a fine felt-tip marker pen or soft (2B) pencil. (I tend to use a pencil because the details can be erased when no longer needed).

3. Use good quality disks for your backups. Those disks you bought at the car boot sale (and weren't they a bargain) - may be good, but more often than not, they will be of second quality or even faulty. A faulty disk may record perfectly well but when you come to read it a few months later, the data may have been partially lost because of bad sectors. I learnt this from bitter experience! Good data doesn't deserve dodgy disks!

4. Don't keep all your backups in the same room as your computer - at least, move one set to another room, keep a set at work or even give one to a friend to look after. This saves the sort of disasters caused by room fires, electrical faults or loss through theft or carelessness.

5. Keep the disks cool (not in the freezer or refrigerator) in a dust-free box and keep your mucky fingers (and those of any other people who might be around) off their recording surfaces.

Tape streamers

The only problem with tape streamers is the cost of the tape drive (and sometimes, the associated control card) but this may be offset by the speed and convenience with which a backup can be carried out -

typically, 2 Mbytes per minute if the tape streamer uses the floppy disk controller or 5 - 6 Mbytes per minute if a dedicated controller is used. Tape streamers have quite reasonable capacities with 80 Mbytes per tape being quite common. The cost per megabyte of files backed up is about a third that of data backed up onto 1.44 Mbyte floppies.

Tape streamers can usually backup your files in one of two ways. The quickest and most economical is for the tape to store an exact image of the directory structure and files on your hard disk - just as DISKCOPY does for floppy disks. The only problem is that you cannot pick out an individual file from this type of backup - which may be inconvenient. The other way is for files to be backed up on an individual basis - this takes longer than the image method and uses more tape space for an equivalent number of files. The advantage is that individual files can be extracted and selectively restored if needed. I like tape streamers because they will backup your system without fuss, and may only need the occasional change of data cartridge while operating.

Tape streamers can be fitted into the case of your computer or, more commonly, used as an external unit. They may use the floppy controller card, or possibly, a dedicated controller card of their own. They use special software to enable them to record your data in an appropriate way which is usually specific to a type of drive, although Central Point Software have included a version of tape backup software in PC Tools.

Tape streamers attached to a floppy controller may require you to disable one of your floppy drives and to configure the tape streamer as that drive. This technique gives a modest throughput of data whereas the transfer of data via a separate interface is much faster and involves less fiddling around with your system. One or two types use the parallel printer port - again, with a modestly fast throughput.

The acceptability and effectiveness of a tape streamer sub-system depends critically upon the software that is provided with your streamer. Until comparatively recently, most of this software was pretty unfriendly for non-expert use and it tended to be unreliable. The commercial pressures of the market place have worked wonders and most software is now reasonably pleasant to use.

CHAPTER 8
DOS versions (and diversions)

One of the least pleasant parts of data recovery is when you realise that your disaster-struck system is running an old version of DOS (the computer operating system) which has exceeded it's 'use-by date'. This is not to say that a machine running MSDOS version 2.11 cannot work satisfactorily but older versions of DOS (pre- MSDOS 5.0) had very limited means of helping you recover from disk disasters and most people would be inclined to give up since they lacked the considerable degree of technical skill required to delve into the innermost recesses of floppy or hard disk data storage.

There are three types of DOS which you might come across. The original Microsoft DOS (hence MSDOS) was devised as a fairly basic and unsophisticated system to help IBM run their new range of PCs in the early 1980s. IBM have their own version of DOS (which they call PCDOS) and like the Microsoft product, it is regularly updated and has almost exactly the same range of features.

Another firm (formerly called Digital Research but recently taken over by Novell) produces a disk operating system called, not surprisingly, DRDOS. Aficionados of DRDOS reckon that it is more user-friendly than either PCDOS or MSDOS but Novell seem to be more interested in networks than in supporting the user base. This is a great pity, because it is a genuinely interesting system. It's currently at version 6.0 and seems to incorporate a lot of those good ideas which the next version of MSDOS ought to/might possibly/definitely should have! DRDOS 5.0 came along at a time when Microsoft's dreadful DOS 4.00 was losing Uncle Bill Gates an awful lot of friends. DOS 4.00 was bug-ridden and awful, and needed a lot of fixes in version 4.01. Few people seem to have had any significant problem with DRDOS 5 and Microsoft lost a lot of custom to their rival.

Version numbers can be a bit confusing, and if you are not sure which one your machine is currently running, type VER {enter} at the command prompt (the A:\> or C:\> on your screen).

If your machine responds with a version number of 5 or more, then smile happily. Unless you are running an IBM PC, your DOS will probably have originated from Microsoft, although it may have additional names and copyright dates if it is a special version (OEM - other equipment manufacturer) produced for firms such as Dell or Compaq. The only drawback to the proliferation of features in more recent DOS versions over the older versions is in the amount of free memory left once they are installed - because of the limitations of the original PC microprocessor (the 8088 CPU), the maximum amount of memory that could be directly used by DOS was restricted to 640 Kbytes. The operating system could take up more than 10 - 20% of this which left less room for programs to use. We are still stuck with this restriction because of the need for downwards compatibility of DOS versions, even though current CPUs such as the 386, 486 and the Pentium can use address very much more memory directly.

As a general rule, you should update your machine's operating system ONLY if by doing so, you will gain a significant improvement in performance or user-friendliness. Older PCs, such as the Amstrad PC 1512 or PC-XT types don't benefit very much from DOS upgrades beyond version 4.00 since they cannot make use of the memory management features of the more recent types. The only significant change is that the size of hard disk partition within which data can be stored is no longer restricted to 32 Mbytes as was the case with all earlier versions.

More recent PCs (particularly the current range of machines which use the 386 or 486 range of CPUs) can benefit quite substantially. It only remains to see what sort of machine you have before deciding upon an upgrade of this nature. You should have some sort of documentation with your computer and a careful read through this should reveal the CPU type number.

If it is an 8086, 8088, V20, V30, V40, 70108 or 70116 your machine is an XT type and you should think carefully about the wisdom of the upgrade path - DOS 4 or greater takes up a great deal of the precious 640k program memory. It may also be impossible to install if your computer does not have a high capacity floppy disk drive since it isn't always possible to obtain the newer versions of DOS on low-capacity disks.

The presence of an 80286 is more helpful since this CPU can manage extended memory (above 1 MByte) if it is installed - and allows you to install the more recent versions of DOS with a sporting chance of reducing the amount of the main 640k memory block which DOS requires - this is because DOS 5 and later versions make use of the extended memory to locate portions of themselves out of the way of normal programs.

The 386 or 486 CPUs are ideally suited for work with DOS 5.0 or more recent versions because of the way in which memory is managed. Quite a number of important programs (such as those which define keyboard language or display attributes and MSDOS) can be exiled to the High Memory Area of the extended memory region and, with a little help from the manual, it's possible to have more than 95% of the 640k available for running programs.

Which DOS?

Data security facilities

DOS 5.0 includes two new commands - UNDELETE and UNFORMAT. The former allows you to restore a file which was deleted by mistake and the latter allows you to recover from an accidental disk format which would normally wipe all data from a floppy or hard disk. It also included a program called MIRROR which saves information about disks and is normally loaded as part of the start-up facility on your machine. UNFORMAT uses information saved by the MIRROR program and can usually restore a disk's structure if it is corrupted.

Formatting is an essential part of data storage in which a pattern of tracks is laid down on the disk before data can be stored on it. The later versions of DOS and DRDOS save a copy of the system information on an unused part of the disk and this can be located as part of the UNFORMAT process. Details of file names, size and location are stored in this way.

In order to use the UNFORMAT facility, it is necessary to format the disk(s) with the built-in FORMAT command when the system is running DOS 5.0. The FORMAT command in earlier versions of DOS does not permit the use of the UNFORMAT command in DOS 5.0.

UNDELETE is a very useful addition since it enables one to restore an accidentally erased file - all too easy to do, particularly if you are in a hurry. UNDELETE uses information kept by the MIRROR program, but it cannot restore a deleted directory nor can it restore a file whose home directory has been removed. If you can find a copy, DRDOS 6.0 has similar utilities - but instead of MIRROR, it has two programs, DISKMAP and DELWATCH which keep track of file and partition information as well as files which have been deleted.

MSDOS 6.0 has the earlier UNFORMAT program and an enhanced UNDELETE command UNDELETE now has three levels of file deletion protection and the MIRROR command no longer exists as such. This version uses the same safe formatting system as DOS 5.0, and lost data can usually be retrieved without too much trouble. The BACKUP program, found on all earlier versions has been enhanced and is also available as a version for use within the Windows environment.

A major addition to DOS is the inclusion of an anti-virus program in both DOS and Windows versions, as well as a virus monitoring program called VSafe. Many users are happy to go for this option, just to have the anti-virus facility

Cost

MSDOS 5.0 is available quite widely for £20 or less now that it has been superseded by MSDOS 6.0 - and DOS 6.0 is available for £55 - 60 or so.   DRDOS 6.0 is much less widely available but I have seen it offered for less than £40.

Upgrading your DOS

MSDOS

Early versions of MSDOS could fit on a single low density 5.25" disk - now the additional utilities are so numerous and large that they require several disks for a full implementation. These versions have many files stored in a compressed format which saves disk space but does mean that the installation process takes longer.

What you'll need:-

1. A genuine copy of MSDOS 5.00 or 6.00 - preferably in a sealed pack with original handbook bearing the Microsoft hologram.   This should ensure that you don't install a virus-infected or unofficially modified version.

The disk size you buy should be the same as the size of your 'A' drive - they are available in both 3.5" and 5.25" formats.   Bear in mind that XT type PC clones like the Amstrad PC1512 and 1640 can only read low density disks and that other similar types of PC are similarly affected unless the system has a floppy disk controller which can cope with high density drives.

PC-ATs - in fact, most modern computers will have at least one high density disk drive fitted.

2. A couple of blank, preferably pre-formatted disks onto which the program can 'uninstall' the existing version of DOS. Label these as Uninstall 1 and Uninstall 2 - you will only need one if you are installing from 3.5" disks.

3. Assuming that your computer has a hard disk, you will need between 2 and 4 megabytes of disk space for installation of the newer DOS versions. If you don't, or there is insufficient space on the hard disk, the installation program will ask you if you want to install on floppy disks. If so, have four 3.5" or seven 5.25" formatted disks of the correct size available for use as prompted.

Installation

If the computer is switched on, turn off the power, wait for a minute. (This is also a sensible anti-virus precaution!)

Insert the Startup (or Install) disk in drive A, and turn on the computer.

When the command prompt (A> or A:\>) appears, type SETUP and press the Enter key. The SETUP process is automated to a considerable extent and is able to find out a lot about your system on its own, but you should inform the program about the type of keyboard layout and language required since the default settings are American. In the UK, this means that the ú sign is not above the figure 3 - instead, you'll get the # (hash) sign!

It is a sensible idea to make an installation of the new version of DOS onto floppy disks - just in case! The advantage of this is that you have a backup of your DOS files in fully expanded form, and most importantly, it gives you a basic 'no-frills' STARTUP disk which you can use to boot-up your system and get it running if the the hard disk fails, or if you need to carry out a major reconfiguration of your system.

The process takes a little longer than for a hard disk and you need a number of formatted and labelled disks of the size as your A drive. Write the following on the labels:

For 3.5" disks   OR   For 5.25" disks

For 3.5" disks	For 5.25" disks
1. Startup/Support	1. Startup
2. Support	2. Shell/Help
3. QBasic/Edit/Utility	3. Shell
4. Supplemental	4. Help
	5. QBasic/Edit
	6. Utility
	7. Supplemental

In this case, run the SETUP program with the following command:

```
a:setup /f
```

which automatically runs the program in floppy installation mode. Always set the 'write-protect' slide or tab on the Startup disk. This will avoid any virus infection, provided your original installation was from virus-free disks.

IF IT DIDN'T WORK - PLEASE READ THIS NOTE

It's just possible that the CMOS information in your machine won't allow the installation because the machine starts up DOS from the hard disk. In this case, re-boot the machine and press whatever keys are needed to get into the CMOS SETUP programs, and alter the disk priority to A, rather than C. (This SETUP program is not the same as the DOS installation program)

DRDOS

Installing DRDOS is very easy since the process starts automatically and prompts you as necessary.

What you'll need

1. A set of DR-DOS 6.0 disks in an appropriate size - preferably in a sealed pack to minimise the chances of viral infection.

2. Sufficient space on your hard disk - about 1.5 - 2 megabytes for a full installation. If you are going to install on floppy disks, make sure you have enough ready-formatted disks available.

I recommend preparing five 5.25" or three 3.5" low density disks, complete with labels.

Installation

Switch off the computer, leave for one minute, then insert the Startup disk.

Turn on the computer and wait for DRDOS to put up the first of it's installation screens. This welcomes you to the wonderful world of DRDOS and tells you what keys you need to use in order to navigate round the system.

The next screen asks you where you wish to install DRDOS. This is where you can opt for a floppy-only installation or put the system on the hard disk.

The setup/configuration process is quite lengthy but you are prompted carefully through it, with sensible defaults. Once the configuration of the system has been carried out, the program then starts installing

DRDOS - asking you if you want to save the old system, and so on.

Making an emergency DOS 'boot' disk

Once the new version of DOS is properly installed on the hard disk, it is wise to make a proper emergency boot disk - the Startup disk will not necessarily do all that you need, particularly if you run with exotic hardware or disk compression in your system.

An emergency disk needs to have the system files (which make the computer work) transferred to it, together with a selected range of 'drivers' and configuration programs. It also needs the AUTOEXEC.BAT and CONFIG.SYS files. which set up many of the operating parameters.

The procedure is quite straightforward.

Take an unformatted disk of the size that fits your A drive. Insert it and from the C:\> prompt, type:

FORMAT a: /s /v (you can use upper or lower case letters)

This prepares the disk and transfers the operating system files to it, and prompts you for a label description (less than 12 characters).

The system files have names such as IO.SYS and MSDOS.SYS, together with COMMAND.COM. If you type DIR A:, the only file name you will see is the last, COMMAND.COM the other two are there, but are hidden from view.

Copy the AUTOEXEC.BAT and CONFIG.SYS from the C drive by typing: copy autoexec.bat a:

and

copy config.sys a:

Examine the files by typing:

```
TYPE AUTOEXEC.BAT   (or CONFIG.SYS)..
```

Look for evidence of special programs such as video, printer or disk drivers in the CONFIG.SYS file and ensure that these are copied to your boot disk.   Similarly, scan the AUTOEXEC file for details of programs which must be run during the startup process, and make sure that these are available.   It is sensible to copy utilities such as CHKDSK, FORMAT and UNFORMAT, UNDELETE and FDISK if there is room.   Do use the highest disk capacity that the floppy drive will take.   DOS 5 and 6 as well as DRDOS 6 need more than the capacity of the 360k 5.25" - I normally use the 1.2 Mbyte or 1.44 Mbyte high density disks, depending upon the size of drive A.

Label the disk appropriately and set the write-protect tab or sticker.   I always try the disk out to make sure it does all that is necessary before making a copy of it.

Check that the disk is in drive A, then type:

```
diskcopy a: a:
```

The utility called DISKCOPY makes a faithful, 'warts and all' copy of the source disk onto an identical capacity destination disk.   It prompts you to swap the source and destination disks several times so make sure that the disks are clearly labelled to avoid confusion.   Put the copy safely aside, just in case it's needed.

CHAPTER 9
Some disk utilities - a brief review

There's no doubting the ingenuity of the authors of packages which claim variously to recover your data, test your disks (usually the hard one) and so on. Some packages can deal correctly with compressed disk partitions while others claim to make your hard disk self-repairing or to include virus detection. In this chapter, I'd like to look at a number of the more readily available packages and to investigate what they do. This is not a 'Which?' guide to software, but a survey of the advertised features which could be helpful.

The mention of a program or package does not necessarily imply an endorsement of that product and the author and publishers cannot be held responsible for any loss or damage caused by the use of these programs.

The most commonly available general disk utilities are Norton and PC Tools, while Disk Technician Gold and Spinrite are broadly representative of the investigation and preventative maintenance side of things. I have not included Mace Utilities, because I have been frustrated in all my attempts to find out more about them. All I know is that there is a 1990 version and disk utilities have moved on a lot since then....

At the time of writing (August 1993), the only one of the general utilities which could deal correctly with compressed drives (such as those produced by Stacker and similar programs and likely to be encountered by users of MSDOS 6) was version 7.0 of Norton Utilities. Where Norton is currently in the lead (in terms of capabilities and gizmos), other programs will follow fairly soon, and if you're thinking about purchasing a copy of Norton or any other program - check out the facilities that their most up-to-date versions have.

PC Tools is currently at version 8 and both Norton and PC Tools seem to be pretty widely available and are often heavily discounted. The discounting may only apply to earlier versions, so be careful when purchasing.

Norton Utilities

Norton has the following programs which are concerned with disks and data:

(for further details, you will have to consult the manuals or one of the books about the package which are currently available)

CALIBRAT - this program is particularly useful since it corrects minor errors of data alignment on hard disks. It carries out a low-level test and format without erasing any data and is particularly handy where a disk suffers from soft errors.

DISKEDIT - this is a very powerful program that enables you to make changes directly to the floppy or hard disk and is an extremely powerful data manipulation tool. Not recommended for beginners or the faint-hearted!

DISKTOOL - one of the most useful programs, which provides a range of special-purpose techniques and tools for recovering data from abused, misused or damaged disks.

FILEFIX - very handy if you have corrupted files from Lotus 1-2-3, Symphony, Excel, Quattro Pro, dBase or WordPerfect - since it can restore their structure. A life-saver for many companies.

IMAGE - this useful program protects your hard disk from an accidental formatting by making a duplicate of all the essential information. This program works in conjunction with the UNFORMAT program and can be run as part of the start-up procedure on your machine at the beginning of every session.

NDIAGS - a set of component test which can check out the whole of your system, or individual items within it such as disk drives. It can run in single-shot, multiple or continuous mode. The last mode is very useful for testing drives which may be suspect.

NDD - this is the Norton Disk Doctor - the saviour of many disks, files and reputations... It finds and corrects errors which occur on both floppy and hard disks, and can also be used to test new disks. This program, on it's own is worth the money you pay for the complete package.

RESCUE - a new facility, which copies the vital setup information for your system from the CMOS RAM and hard disk and puts it, with system information, on a backup disk. This information could be handy if your system configuration information was lost.

SFORMAT - This is the safe formatting program which some people prefer to the FORMAT program provided with DOS. It adds a number of features to the process of disk formatting which makes it inherently less unfriendly for non-experts.

SMARTCAN - This is a useful program which modifies the way in which files are deleted/erased, so that your chances of recovering them are improved.

SPEEDISK - This helps maximise the performance of your machine by housekeeping and re-organising your disk. It sorts directories, de-fragments files and arranges data on disk for fast access.

UNERASE - self explanatory, but another excellent program that provides tools for both automated and manual recovery of programs and data files that you have accidentally deleted.

UNFORMAT - as it's name suggests, this reverses the destructive effects of an unwanted FORMAT on your hard disk and allows files to be recovered.

PC Tools

This is a very comprehensive package which contains the following files which are relevant to this book:

COMPRESS - in spite of it's name, this program actually de-fragments a hard disk by re-arranging scattered data clusters. It's nearest equivalent in Norton is SPEEDISK.

CPBACKUP - this is a great improvement on the DOS BACKUP program and permits the use of tape streamers as well as floppy disks for hard disk backup.

DATAMON - a program which monitors the way in which files are deleted so that their recovery can be facilitated. It's very sophisticated and works at several levels of security.

DISKFIX - this is similar in function to Norton Disk Doctor and Calibrate, with some Diagnostics thrown in as well. A very useful program.

FILEFIX - just like it's counterpart in Norton, this one will recover many dBase and similar files, as well as Lotus 1-2-3 and Symphony. The current version doesn't recover WordPerfect files.

INSTALL - in addition to it's main task of installing PC Tools on your hard disk, this program produces a Recovery disk, with the same sort of facilities as the Rescue disk from Norton. The kernel of the recovery disk is the REBUILD program, which reconstructs those bits of your hard disk and system information that have been lost.

MIRROR - this operates in the same way as Norton's IMAGE program and backs up the FAT, root directory and boot record.

PCFORMAT - this operates in a similar way to SFORMAT in Norton. It is far superior in operation to the DOS FORMAT command.

UNDEL - as might be expected, this program recovers deleted files - and does so even more readily if one or other of the DATAMON options is in operation.

UNFORMAT - another recovery program which will reverse the effects of formatting on a hard disk - just like the Norton version.

VDEFEND - one of the unique features of PC Tools. This is a virus scanner which remains resident in memory and warns if any of the tell-tale indications of a virus are present. Currently, it checks for more than 400 types of virus and particularly monitors any attempts on the part of any program to carry out the viruses favourite trick - namely to carry out a destructive, low-level format of the hard disk. Norton's Antivirus is in a separate package.

Both Norton and PC Tools have many other facilities which would make either one of them a good package to have on your computer.

Disk Technician Gold

Disk Technician Gold (DTG) is a sophisticated hard disk maintenance package which can carry out a wide range of tests and a fair range of disk repairs when required - it does most of this quite unobtrusively, beavering away in the background.

It has a number of useful features which would commend it users to whom data security would be important - for example it can detect and correct soft errors, detect intermittent errors and warn if it's tests predict an imminent disk failure. You could then backup your disk before disaster strikes.

A major feature of this package is it's ability to recover data and carry out a full reconstruction - which is said to be better than either Norton or PC Tools. I haven't had a chance to test this out - luckily! The package also performs all read/write operations on a hard disk in a fail-safe mode, so that in the event of a power failure, nothing would be lost or destroyed. This, while not unique, is an important feature.

In common with the other programs mentioned, DTG has diagnostics and de-fragmentation abilities, and a virus prevention program. I must admit to being a little irritated by the last feature, which seemed a lot more intrusive than the PC Tools or Dr Solomon's programs.

The program has some particularly good features, like, for example, it's ability to cope with all manner of hard disk controllers and drives and the care taken to ensure that drives (such as IDE types) which would suffer from a low level format are excluded and cannot be formatted by mistake.

Perhaps not the best program for a home PC user, but it could be very valuable in the office.

Spinrite is an older but broadly similar program to DTG - but lacks some of the latter's clever facilities. I first came across it in it's early, public domain times and was quite impressed with later developments as a hard disk tester. I suspect that some of it's excellent features, such as variable depth pattern testing have been imitated in other, more recent programs but I still find it an extremely useful program to have around when I'm dealing with older disks. It does seem to find the errors other programs miss, and for that reason, and the ease with which one is able to suspend and restart scanning operations, I like it.

CHAPTER 10
Disk Disasters - and what does and doesn't cause them...

Disk failures can occur as a result of a number of factors, some of which are the result of the disks itself, others because of the disk drive and a few to external influences such as people or hot coffee.

Let's look at some of them:

Media deterioration

The magnetic coating on a floppy or hard disk is usually pretty reliable, but there may be minor imperfections on the disk surface where data storage is impaired because of a fault in the magnetic material. Over a period of several months or years, the ability of these areas to retain data declines, and errors result. This leads to an increase in the number of bad sectors on the disk, and also to data loss.

Magnetic impairment

Data is stored on disk as patterns of magnetic flux reversals which are produced as a result of the changing electrical currents in the read/write heads. Over a period of several months or years, depending upon the type of disk, the strength of these markings will fade and reading data in this state is a little chancy, with an increasing chance of failures. DOS tries to re-read faulty data 30 times in a row before giving an error message, so you won't necessarily know that you've got a problem until it hits you! In my experience, low coercivity disks (generally the double-density types) tend to fade more easily than high coercivity types, but data is generally readable for at least 4 or 5 years. The cure for this is to copy the data onto another disk.

Electro-mechanical alignment

Disk drives are electro-mechanical devices, but thankfully, electrical problems are very rare. What does happen from time to time, particularly with older types of drive which use stepper motors, is that the actuator that moves the heads across the disk surface may get out of alignment either through wear and tear or temperature fluctuations. In extreme cases, the heads fail to cover any data tracks at all, and nothing can be read from the disk.

Hard disks can suffer from a problem called platter wobble. This happens when a disk has been in service for a long time and the spindle bearings become so worn that the platter wobbles very slightly. This may be sufficient to impair correct writing and reading of data and could also contribute to the next type of problem.

Head crashes

When a read/write head (which is quite small) touches the surface of a hard disk platter which is running at 3600 r.p.m., it may flick off a small particle of the magnetic material. This will cause a data failure in that area, and the process may also cause physical damage to the head which may render it unable to read or write data. If this damage occurs on the first track of the disk (whimsically called track (or cylinder) 0), the disk is probably unusable since track 0 is where its file allocation tables, partition table and root directory are kept. Head crashes are also caused by bumping or knocking a drive that is switched on.

Electrical or mechanical failure

Electrical failures, such as motor which burns out, are quite rare and, in economic terms, there's not a lot one can do to recover data from a drive which has this problem. A more common fault is where an individual component on a drive controller board fails. In this case, it may be possible to redeem the situation by fitting a replacement board, but, unless the replacement is second-hand, and readily available, it may cost more than the drive or data are worth.

Controller errors

All-electronic assemblies are normally highly reliable, once they have been used for a while (the so-called 'burn-in' period). If they are going to fail, they usually do so early on. Occasionally, thermal cycling can cause problems with components which are socketed on the board and this may interfere with system tolerances and data errors can result.

Electrical surges

If you happen to live or work in an area where your neighbour uses an arc-welder or similar equipment which takes a lot of power, you may be troubled with voltage 'spikes' on the power supply. These can be reduced by a surge-limiting plug and the computer's power supply may also have further surge-limiting capabilities but - there is a slight chance that an unusually fast or heavy surge may occur then you are writing data to disk. In which case, you might have a data problem. Lightning strikes on power lines can cause similar problems but I haven't come across anyone who has had drive electronics damaged by this cause! If you don't have a surge-protection plug on your system - do get one. They can save you a great deal of trouble if your mains power supply is at all 'noisy'.

Software problems

This could range from some of the nastier problems associated with 'viruses' to a piece of software which does unkind things to your hard disk and it's contents. The latter sometimes occurs because someone has accidentally re-named a program so that the program's true purpose is obscured. I had one such case where a directory-sort program which a friend gave me, turned out to be an extremely unforgiving disk formatter! Very nasty if it happens to you.

Operator error

Well, we're all human.... It is remarkably easy, when tired or fed-up to erase all the files, format a disk or even to take a floppy disk out of the drive while it is being written to!   The unfortunate effect of the last exercise is that the file's directory entry is not updated until the complete file is written - simply because its only then that the system knows how much space to set aside. Sometimes, directories may be damaged.   Rather than press the reset button or CTRL+ALT+DEL, try CTRL+C since this will often allow an orderly close down of the processes.   Only re-boot if absolutely necessary and NEVER as a panic measure.

Let's now look at floppy and hard disks in more detail:

Floppy disks

There are a number of things that you should never do to floppy disks. Most people are fairly kind to floppies, others are a bit forgetful but some should never be let anywhere near floppy disks!

Let's look at some of the more obvious areas for potential grief and 'tears before bed-time'.

1. Clean hands - but don't touch the sensitive surface of your disks even if you think that your hands are squeaky clean. Fingers carry small amounts of natural oils, dirt, dust etc. and this is easily transferred. Dirt will then adhere and, after a while, the data may become irrecoverable until the disk is cleaned properly. This is not particularly easy.

2. Don't bend the disk or, as one bright spark did in the local library, stapled the disk into the book so that it shouldn't get lost - definitely not a sensible thing to do!

3. Be sensibly careful how you handle the disk - for example, don't write on a 5.25" disk label with a ball-point pen or hard pencil. It WILL damage the disk, so use a fine point fibre-tip pen.

4. Don't throw the disk around or use it as a frisbee

5. Don't use a floppy as a stand for hot drinks. The heat reduces the strength of the recorded magnetic field, as does leaving your floppies or cassettes in the sun or near a radiator. Remember that a car can get very hot on a summer's day, as can a window sill and your precious data will be corrupted all too easily.....

6. Keep your disks well away from magnetic fields and dust. Dust particles can cause data errors as the disk drive heads become clogged.

The first four of these rules are pretty basic and common sense should guide you in your actions.

It's perhaps less clear why heat whether from a mug of coffee or from the sun should be so destructive but it all relates to the Curie temperature, above which a magnetisable medium suddenly loses its magnetic properties. A really hot mug of coffee has a temperature just above the Curie point, and 5.25" disks in a car on a hot summer's day can get very warm and will approach this temperature. The overall effect is to cause total or patchy loss of data. Nasty!

Magnetism is pretty insidious. Tools can become magnetic after periods of use and some (particularly screwdrivers) are purposely magnetised so that they can pick up or retain screws and bolts. There are other sources of magnetism around the place and you should take care of your disks in these situations since data loss can occur either at once or after a long-ish period of proximity, depending upon the strength of the magnetism.

Typical examples of magnetism in domestic and workplace situations are as follows:

Old style (dial, not press-button) telephones.

Loudspeakers

Electric motors

TV sets and monitors (Colour types in particular)

Magnetic letters (children's) or magnetically backed paper tidies and desk organisers.

Coils of mains cable carrying a heavy current

Screwdrivers and other small tools

The most vulnerable disks, even to low levels of magnetism, are the 5.25" low density types. Magnetic damage is cumulative, and low levels of exposure which cause slight damage can eventually end up with an unreadable disk. The 3.5" types seem rather more resistant to this sort of damage because of the higher coercivity of the magnetic material.

Modern press-button telephones with an electronic 'ringer' are fairly safe when in fairly intimate contact with floppy disks but old style dial telephones have a powerful electromagnet and striker which rings the bell and this will wipe (degauss) any disk in close proximity.
Loudspeakers contain magnets (the type used in large speaker systems are sometimes very powerful).

Electric motors also generate quite powerful magnetic fields ....

Colour TV sets and monitors have a built-in coil around the tube which removes any stray magnetism from the 'shadow mask' inside the picture tube when the TV/monitor is first switched on. If this isn't done, there is a strong chance that residual magnetism in the shadow mask at the front of the picture tube can bend electron beams to give odd colours and poor focus. Disks within a foot or so of a monitor can be affected since every time the monitor is switched on, there is a massive surge of electricity in the de-gaussing coil which rapidly sinks to zero aa the process is terminated. This sort of treatment can reduce the intensity of stored magnetic signals on disk or tape and is both cumulative and irreversible.

It may seem surprising to include screwdrivers and other small tools but these are made of steel and under certain circumstances, can become magnetised sufficiently to present a danger to low-density disks. Tools and disks should be kept well apart. The same applies to reels of extension cable - one user lost several months' data when an extension cable reel was accidentally placed on a box of disks, connected to an electric heater and the current switched on. The alternating magnetic field was sufficient to de-gauss all the disks - immediately!

Hard Disks

Hard disks are less likely to be affected by magnetic problems but, because of their mechanical construction and the very small clearance between the read/write heads and the disk platters, any undue shock or vibration can cause damage to the disk platters, heads or both. Most modern hard disks are reasonably well-protected against mechanical shock when they are switched off since the read/write heads are automatically parked in a safe zone. Older disks do not always have this safety feature and unless the heads are parked before the machine is switched off, any mechanical shock may cause damage and consequent data loss.

Most users know that dropping a computer on the floor would cause serious damage to any hard disk, whether it's in use or switched off. What is not generally appreciated is that even a relatively gentle knock or bump can cause damage to a disk which is in use, and this could be caused quite easily by moving the computer while it is switched on, or even by dropping something on the desk next to the computer.

An Old Wives' Tale .....

A significant number of computer users regularly take their lap-tops and disks through airports and get significantly worried about the effects of the X ray machine on the contents of the computer or floppy disks. Forget it.   There is no danger at all.

..... and a Cautionary Tale

The disks must go through the X ray machine and NOT through some sort of metal detector.

If in doubt, ask (politely).

Metal detectors are sometimes used at airports but are more often seen in libraries, where they are used to detect unauthorised removal of metal-tagged library books.   Metal detectors emit a magnetic field and this is sometimes sufficient to corrupt floppy disks (they can also upset heart pacemakers as well!).

X ray machines also emit radiation but the only effect that would be noticed as far as a floppy disk is concerned would be an imperceptible warming - nothing like as much as would be caused by leaving the disk on a sunny windowsill for a couple of hours.

The wrong disk

One disaster which can strike the unwary is to try to read a correctly formatted 5.25" 80 track high density disk in a 40 track low density drive. The disk will be unreadable and will result in a 'General Failure' error message on screen.

This is not likely to happen with low density disks since these are readable in the high density drive. The media selector sensor in a high density 3.5" drive will, if the sensor is enabled, automatically sense the presence of a 720K disk, and it will be correctly dealt with.

If the media sensor isn't working or you have a PS/2 machine, this may allow you to format a 720K disk to 1.44M. The format may have proceeded normally, with no bad sectors, but disks formatted in this way may well exhibit random read or write failures. These occur in a sporadic fashion and may manifest themselves after a few weeks or even as much as a year. You will get the same effect on a system which has a correctly enabled media sensor if you're tempted to punch out the media selector hole on a 720k disk. If you do - then you deserve all the trouble you get!

The media sensor is usually enabled with a jumper (a tiny piece of plastic and metal) on the drive electronics board.

If an attempt is made to format a 5.25" low density disk to high density, several hundred thousand bytes of bad sectors are reported - under these circumstances, most folk would not use the disk. As mentioned previously, it is possible to use an incorrectly formatted 3.5" disk and provided that the data is re-read and re-written from time to time, it will not be immediately obvious that there is likely to be a problem with the disk. The problem arises because the low density disks have a more sensitive magnetic coating and if this is recorded with the high level of write current that is used for the lower sensitivity high density disks. The recording process produces magnetic flux reversals (domains) which are very closely spaced when recorded in high density mode.

Over a period of time, depending upon the quality of the disk coating, the magnetic domains may interact and cancel each other out, thus yielding a series of unreadable sectors on the disk.

Damaged disks

Disks can be damaged in a number of ways - such as by being bent or creased - maybe your friendly postman did this for you!   Coffee or other drinks, when spilt on a disk, can cause problems as well, but there are a number of ways of sorting things out.   If drying the disk thoroughly doesn't help, more desperate measures may be needed.

In both eventualities, you need a brand new disk of the same size (and type) and a craft knife or safety razor blade.   Very carefully and neatly, slit one side of the new disk's jacket or prise apart the disk jacket and remove the contents.

Take the damaged disk and proceed as follows:

Spilt drink:

Slit the disk jacket along one side or prise it apart (carefully) and extract the contents (very carefully).   Wash the disk with cold water, allowing to soak for a few minutes if the deposit had dried. Wash again and do not rub the disk.   Allow it to dry without heat and then carefully insert it in the new jacket - getting it the right way up in the case of 5.25" disks - a bit of trial and error here...

Bent or creased:

Slit or prise open the disk jacket as before and establish if the disk is intact.   If so, transfer it to the new jacket and you should have no trouble. If the disk itself is bent, then it is sensible to attempt to flatten it under a heap of heavy books for a time before attempting put it into the new jacket in order to read it.

In both cases, immediately copy the disk using DISKCOPY onto a fresh disk. If this doesn't work, then you probably have the disk in upside down - so carefully turn it the correct way up and try again. Keep the slit jacket but throw away the damaged disk.

This should work in most situations but will not recover data from severely physically damaged disks due to such happenings as pin-holes, cigarette ash burns or disks contaminated with non water-soluble residues.

Drive problems

Undoubtedly, modern disk drives are pretty reliable but sometimes, physical problems while reading or writing disks can lead to an apparent disk disaster.

One of the commonest problems with 5.25" disks has been mentioned earlier and is due to the narrower track width of the 80 track drive compared with the track width of the low density drive. Overall, this means that it is possible to bet 80 track width data overwritten onto a 40 track pattern and this causes severe confusion and the disk cannot be read in the low density drive.

Disk drives, particularly when they are used a lot in dusty environments, can get dirty and dust and dirt accumulates on the read/write heads. Usually, an occasional prophylactic with a wet cleaning kit works wonders. A special disk dampened with a cleaning agent such as alcohol or similar solvent is inserted into the drive and the drive is activated. You might be surprised at how dirty some drives are but don't go mad with the cleaner disk since this can cause excessive wear to the read/write heads.

Alignment problems can occur if the disk drive has suffered some abuse in the past - such as being dropped. In this case, there may be difficulties in reading disks from other systems but disks written to on your system can be read by it. They probably won't work with other systems either! The read/write head misalignment problem can be corrected sometimes if you have the appropriate software and alignment diskette but it is expensive and not to be recommended for the average user. Buy a new disk drive - it's cheaper and less of a problem - use the old one to read in your disks to the system before junking it.

It is almost impossible to insert a 3.5" disk incorrectly into it's drive, but quite easy to do the same for a 5.25". Put it in upside down and it will not work, and neither will it work properly if the disk is clamped into place in a lop-sided fashion. This will usually result in a 'General Failure' message but normally, removal and careful re-insertion is all that is required to put matters right.

CHAPTER 11
Data storage

All computer users need to store their programs or data for future use and various methods have been tried. Temporary storage in the computer's memory, either in the conventional RAM or a RAM disk is possible, but the data is lost when the machine is switched off. For permanent storage, early computers produced punched paper tape which could be read into the computer at a later date; paper tapes were fairly fragile and tore easily. Punched cards could be used although these were less convenient (a long program used lots of cards and the cards were easily damaged, muddled or mislaid). Magnetic data storage was first used with mainframe computers and data was stored in 7 or 9 tracks on half-inch wide magnetic tape (which could be removed for storage) or on large, magnetically coated disks (the precursors of modern hard disks).

Early PCs used audio cassette tapes and these were most convenient for data storage since they were quite cheap and readily available. The writing and reading of data (recording and playback) could be carried out on a domestic cassette player, but was frustratingly slow.

Tapes, whether paper or magnetic, can only contain data which is recorded in a sequential fashion. The drawback of this method is that data cannot then be accessed at random since there is usually no means of deciding exactly where on the tape that the desired program or data is located, unless just one program or data set was present. Punched cards suffered from this problem to a lesser extent because the details of the punching were printed out along the top of each card and it was possible (but sometimes time-consuming) to find the start and end of the desired material by a manual search.

The development of floppy disks revolutionised data storage and retrieval since it became possible to locate individual programs, results or data sets (known as files) on the disk because the details of each file's location and size were stored on the same disk and could be accessed very rapidly.

Early floppy disks were 8" in diameter, later on, 5.25" and 3.5" types were produced and the currently popular standard is for the 3.5" size. 3" disks were used in some cases but the size was never popular except in Amstrad PCW computers.

Recent developments have included various forms of optical disk drive (such as the CD-ROM) which have very high storage capacities but most of these cannot be used to record your data directly. Thus for most systems, the data storage facility is likely to be a form of magnetic storage.

Data storage on floppy disks is achieved through the use of a flexible plastic disk on which is deposited a thin layer of iron oxide (with other additives to improve it's magnetic performance). The disk is kept within a protective case and is spun at a constant speed (either 300 or 360 revolutions per minute) in the disk drive. The 8" type (now largely obsolete) and the obsolescent 5.25" types are enclosed in a very flexible envelope (hence the term 'floppy disk') but the 3.5" (and 3") are contained in a rigid plastic case.

How floppy disks are constructed

The two commonly used sizes of floppy disk differ greatly in their construction although they both use the same plastic base material (mylar) which is coated with a magnetic mixture. The larger 5.25" type is flexible, contained within a plastic jacket and with several holes of varying sizes and functions.

The largest hole (in the middle) is known as the hub access hole and enables the disk to locate on a plastic hub within the drive. It is centred and clamped on to this hub when in use: the hole is usually re-inforced with a thin plastic ring but not all high density disks have this addition. Below the hub hole is a long slot which is referred to as the media access hole; the drive heads move over this area of the disk and it is also an area in which careless handling may cause damage to the disk surface.

On either side of the media access hole are two small notches which relieve strain on the disk and prevent warping. Towards the top right of the disk, about an inch from the top edge is a rectangular notch. This is referred to as the write-enable notch and functions as a write-protect device when it is taped over with an opaque sticker. If left exposed, the disk may be read from or, more critically, written to, but if obscured, the disk may only be read from.

To the right of the hub hole is a small round hole. If the disk is rotated within it's jacket, a corresponding hole can be found on the plastic disk. This is the index hole which is used to locate the starting point of all sectors on the disk. Some (now obsolete) systems used disks which had several (10 or so) index holes and these were referred to as hard sectored disks. Modern disks have a single index hole and are known as soft sectored Hard sectored disks cannot be used in place of soft sectored ones and vice-versa.

Occasionally, you may come across disks with no write-enable notch. These are often used to distribute software and cannot be erased or over-written. They are not suitable for any other use unless a suitable notch is cut out. Some floppy disks may have two index holes and two write-enable notches. These were for certain (now obsolete) single-sided disk drives and were reversible - you turned them over to access the other side. The disks can be used conventionally, but it is as well to tape over the left-hand write-enable slot.

The 3.5" type is constructed very differently, with a rigid plastic case which protects the disk inside. This contributes to the ability of these disks to record data more densely than the 5.25" type.

A metal shutter covers the media access hole and is automatically opened by inserting the disk into the drive. The shutter closes automatically when the disk is removed from the drive and the sensitive media is protected from dusty environments or sticky fingers.

There is a square hole (on the lower left hand side of the disk), known as the write-enable/protect hole whose function is carried out by a plastic slider. If the hole is covered by the slider, then the disk can be written to or files can be erased. If the hole is open, then the disk is write-protected. Some disks have a second square hole on the lower right hand side which acts as a media-density selector. If the hole is not present, the disk is low density and if it is there, then you have a high density disk. In the latter case, there may also be a stylised HD logo just to the right of the shutter.

On the under-side of all 3.5" disks, there is a large central hole with a metal disk which is bonded to the magnetic medium. This is referred to as the centre hub and when the disk is inserted in a drive, the hub engages with a mating device on the disk drive motor to ensure correct alignment. At the top of the disk, on each side are 2 locating holes which help keep the disk in alignment within the drive.

The disk drive contains some electronics which control the rate of rotation of the disk and the data is read from or written to the floppy disk by a movable read/write head. All modern disk drives can read and write to both sides of a floppy disk while some earlier ones can only cope with one side. The read/write head is an electromagnetic device.

The oxide-coated surface of the disk is rotated past the read/write head and in an analogous fashion to a tape recorder, changes in the digital electrical signal fed to the read/write head are converted into changes in magnetic flux on the disk. The same read/write head will pick up changes in the magnetic pattern on a pre-recorded disk and relay these as an electrical signal. Data is recorded onto the disk as a pattern of magnetic changes and will remain in place for several years unless the disk is re-written to or formatted.

When it is first manufactured, the magnetisable particles on the surface of the disk are aligned at random. When data is written to a disk, the passage of a small electric current through the read/write head causes a localised magnetic field to be set up which aligns the particles close to it into a particular direction. This direction is maintained even when the disk is removed from the disk drive and is referred to as a semi-permanent state which can either be changed through the agency of the read/write head, or by the use of a powerful magnet. The particles which have been aligned are referred to as a flux - a magnetic field with a particular direction - and changing data results in a change in magnetic flux - that is, from one direction to the opposite direction (analogous to an on- and off- or binary state). Data consists of changes in flux direction (known as flux reversals) and, as recorded on disks, a flux in one direction is known as logic 0 and in the opposite direction, as logic 1. Flux reversals are brought about by changing the direction of current flow in the read/write head, thus writing data on the disk surface.

Within a computer, the representation of data is in a binary (0 or 1) form and each 0/1 is referred to as a bit. When data consisting of a stream of 1's and 0's is transferred to the disk controller, it ends up by being converted into a series of flux reversals and the 0 or 1 pattern is represented by one or other particle alignment. A typical data stream consists of strings of 0 and 1 bits such as 10010011.

To make the most efficient use of the magnetic medium, it is necessary to encode the data. Two basic forms of data encoding are in use - one, MFM (Modified Frequency Modulation) is used for both floppy and hard disks while the other, known as RLL (Run Length Limited) is only used for hard disks. RLL encoding packs more information on a disk but is prone to errors. Developments of the RLL technique such as ARLL (used for modern IDE (Integrated drive electronics) hard disks are much more reliable.

For the encoded data on the disk to be of any use at all, it must first be retrieved.   If the read/write head passes over an area of disk where there is a flux reversal, this will generate a minute electrical signal which signals a 0 or 1 state.   A series of such reversals must then be decoded to provide a suitable input of data to the computer.   The amplitude of the signal is much smaller than that which was used to generate the initial pattern on the disk.   There are error-checking routines built into the data transfer process which ensure that data storage and retrieval is as free from problems as possible.

For a disk to work correctly in a computer, it is necessary to prepare it's surface to receive data.

On a conventional gramophone record, the music is recorded along both sides of a continuous, fine groove which starts at the edge and finishes near the centre.   On a floppy disk, data is recorded on separate circular, concentric tracks (sometimes called cylinders), normally 40 or 80 on each side.   This pattern of tracks is laid down by the process known as formatting - in addition, the formatting process divides each track into a number of sectors (usually 9, 15 or 18) and sets aside space for a file directory and two copies of a file allocation table (FAT) in which information on the location and size of all files is held.   There are two copies of the FAT in case one becomes damaged.   Information in the FATs is updated when an entry is made in the directory area by the removal or addition of a file.

The amount of data which can be held on a disk depends upon it's size, the number of tracks on it's surface and the density with which the data is written to the disk.   The main features of double-sided floppy disks are tabulated below, and show that, with the exception of the original PC and PC-XT 40 track disks, all modern floppy disks used in PCs have 80 tracks per side.   Conventionally, the lower surface of the disk (the side opposite to the label) is first written to, then the upper.

Disk size	Tracks per side	Sectors per track	Formatted storage capacity	
			nominal	actual
5.25"	40	9	360Kbytes	362,496 bytes (354K)
5.25"	80	15	1.2 Mbytes	1,213,952 bytes (1.186M)
3.5"	80	9	720Kbytes	730,112 bytes (713K)
3.5"	80	18	1.44Mbytes	1,457,664 bytes (1.424M)
3.5"	80	36	2.88Mbytes	2,915,328 bytes (2.848M)

When a floppy disk is prepared using the DOS FORMAT command, two separate processes are carried out. Initially, the disk is physically formatted to lay down the pattern of tracks and sectors (the low level format) and then logically formatted to lay down the FATs and directory structure. Formatting also discovers if any areas of the disk are unable to retain data correctly (these are known as bad sectors and are marked so that data will not be stored there). Modern disks are normally very reliable if formatted to the correct density and disks which show any bad sectors should be disposed of since they are not likely to be reliable for long term data storage.

The next table looks at media types (not the publishing or TV sort!) and their characteristics. These characteristics determine how many tracks can be safely formatted on a disk, how densely the data can be encoded, and what strength of magnetism is needed to produce the best flux reversal - since too strong a magnetic pulse can affect the long-term stability of the stored data.

This table also shows the all-important track-width parameter. This is particularly critical for 5.25" disks since it is quite possible to use both types in an AT- type machine, but with great care. More of this later....

The idea is that for a standard 5.25" 40 track disk, the read/write head records a pattern no more than 0.33 mm wide on each track, and that the recorded pattern is separated from the pattern on the adjacent tracks by a thin, guard area with no recording. With the 80 track disk, the recorded zone is half as wide, and has the same narrow unrecorded areas on either side. The 3.5" disks have an even narrower recorded zone per cylinder.

A quick glance at the table shows that there are major differences between all the types of disk.

The type, thickness and coercivity of the media are important - for example, the lowest density disks (40 track 5.25") have a low coercivity which means that it requires a lower level of magnetic field strength to make a proper recording than, for example, the high density 80 track 5.25" types. The thickness of the coating is quite important since the thinner coatings tend to suffer less degradation over a long period of storage than the low coercivity high thickness types.

The 40 track disks are more sensitive to magnetic disturbance than the higher density types, but the trade-off is that it is easier and cheaper to make such disks.

The 2.88 megabyte format floppy disk is currently supported by DOS 5.0 and 6.0 and probably represents the limit of magnetic floppy disk data storage with our present technology. The disks are several times more expensive than 1.44M disks and are not, at present, cost-effective. Most PC-AT clones have 1.44M drives and these will not read the higher density format. It is possible to format 720K or 1.44M disks correctly in a 2.88M drive, or 720K disks in a 1.44M drive. This is because of the identical umber of tracks and track dimensions in this drive size.

To record a signal on a high density disk, the drive has to generate a stronger magnetic field than for a lower density disk. If a low density disk is to be prepared (formatted) in a high density disk drive, then the drive must have the capacity to provide a Reduced Write Current mode which produces the lower strength of magnetic field which these disks need.

Media characteristics

5.25"

	360K/40 track	1.2M/80 track
Tracks per inch	48	96
Track width (mm)	0.330	0.160
Recording density (Bits per inch)	5,876	9,646
Media doping	Ferrite	Cobalt/Ferrite
Coercivity (oersteds)	300	675
Media thickness ( )	2.5	1.3
Media density type	Double (DD)	High (HD)

(1 micron = 1/1000 mm)

3.5"

	720K	1.44M	2.88M
Tracks per inch	135	135	135
Track width (mm)	0.115	0.115	0.115
Recording density (Bits per inch)	8,717	17,434	34,868
Media doping	Cobalt/Ferrite	Cobalt/Ferrite	Barium/Ferrite
Coercivity (oersteds)	660	720	750
Media thickness ( )	1.9	0.84	2.0
Media density type	Double (DD)	High (HD)	Extra-High (ED)

With all magnetic media, there is a loss of magnetic field strength over time. What this means in practice is that over a period of a few years from their production, you will not notice any significant problems when attempting to read backup or archive disks. Most modern media are classed as high-retentivity which means that the pattern of magnetic flux change which represents your data will be around in good condition for a long time.

Just how retentive your disks are is a little difficult to predict but I recently (1992) was able to read and copy some data from floppy disks which were written in 1983. The best advice is to make regular, timed backups of important archive material at intervals of a year or two and to keep the disks cool and away from any significant magnetic fields. If you intend keeping your hard disk for a long time, it would be wise to refresh data and program files every year or so by carrying out a complete backup, refreshing the format and then restoring the contents.

Very few hard disks are more than 7 or 8 years old since they tend to suffer terminal mechanical or electronic failure at some time. In general, a hard disk used for 8 hours a day, 5 days a week should last for at least 5 years (roughly 10,000 hours use) if it is reasonably well looked after. In fact, a new disk drive can, and occasionally does, fail within a few weeks of installation whilst others go on for many more thousands of hours.

If you buy a second-hand disk, you may not know how long it has been used for and consequently, what it's lifespan might be and the price you pay should reflect this. Any disk should be backed up on a regular basis and this should be sufficient to cover you in the event of a catastrophic hard disk failure.

Similarly, most users upgrade their machine from time to time and are likely to purchase a new hard disk if only to increase their on-line storage. The backup will enable you to transfer data to the new disk and the original disk may be kept as a spare or sold to defray the costs of the upgrade. So - not many people (apart from enthusiasts) will actually encounter a disk breakdown.

Drive life can be prolonged by reducing thermal cycling - which is a trendy way of saying that a system should not be switched off and on too many times since the temperature changes cause considerable wear and tear - both on the drive and other electronic components in the computer. Disk drives should also be as well-ventilated as is reasonably possible since a cool drive will undergo less mechanical and electronic stress than a hot one.

Problems, problems...

If you try to format a low coercivity disk in a drive which is designed for high coercivity media, or vice-versa,you may be in for a shock. A 360K floppy will format (unreliably and with many bad sectors) in a high density drive. A 1.2M floppy will not format properly in a low density drive - in fact, it probably won't format at all - but there have to be exceptions! A colleague of mine once managed the nearly impossible in an Amstrad PC and was able to format a high density disk in the standard low density 40 track drive. What was worse, he used it successfully for several months before it died. I was unable to recover anything from the disk....

If you have an AT type of machine, the 5.25" drive is almost always a 1.2M type and you can format low density disks if you use the correct switch in the format line.

For DOS 3.3 you use:

```
FORMAT A: /n:9 /t:40
```

DOS 4.0 to 6.0 are delightfully simple - use:

```
FORMAT A: /f:360
```

There is a potential problem, due to the narrow track width of the high density drive but it's unlikely to occur if the disk is new and unformatted. If I need to use such a disk, I scramble it's particles by careful use of a powerful magnet!   If you have a disk which was formatted in a 40 track drive, and you re-format it using the low density switch in an 80 track drive, some of the original recording will be left behind, unerased. The end result is a disk which may not be readable on any machine since a 40 track drive will pick up a mixed signal since it's head width is greater than the newly formatted tracks, and an 80 track drive might pick up a signal which is too weak.   The latter problem doesn't often occur, except with drives which have alignment problems.

As a general rule, low density floppy disks should only be formatted and written to using low density, 40 track drives.

With the introduction of the 1.44M drive in 1987, as part of the PS/2 range, and it's rapid adoption by clone manufacturers, the future of the 3.5" drive type was assured since it was clearly a more sensible way of storing data than the cumbersome and vulnerable 5.25" types. As usual, media costs were high and some bright sparks found that if a small hole was punched in the case, opposite the write protect slide, the lower density (and cheaper) 720K type could be formatted to 1.44M.   A few bad sectors might be seen but it worked.....

The drawback was that the high capacity drive was fooled into thinking that the disk was a 1.44M type, and capable of taking the much higher recording current.   The data was there, but because of the high flux density, adjacent flux reversals began to interact and cancel each other. Over a period of a few days, this tendency is almost negligibly small, but after 6 - 9 months, much data is lost. Tough!   If you've done this, then you deserved all the hassle you got..... (It's happened to me!)

If you are lucky, a piece of opaque tape over the drilled media density selector hole, followed by a standard 720K format will sort things out but sometimes the high level of recording is 'burned in' and you may meed a bulk eraser to scramble the disk prior to a new formatting at the correct density.   The IBM PS/2 has a lot to answer for.....   This machine does not check the type of media by interrogating the media sensor device which is built in to most high density drives. The media sensor sets the appropriate level of write current and operating mode according to whether there is a hole (high density) or no hole.

The correct way to ensure that a 720K disk is correctly formatted in a 1.44M drive is to type either

```
FORMAT d: /n:9 /t:80 (for DOS 3.3)
```

or (for DOS 4.0 to 6.0)

```
FORMAT d: /f:720
```

(d: refers to drive A: or B:)

DOS versions earlier than 3.3 cannot support the 1.44M drive type unless an intelligent floppy controller is fitted.

If you do not specify (using either of the above methods) the disk capacity, then the drive will attempt to format the disk to the maximum possible (1.44 M). This is not good news since it is quite difficult to erase a 3.5" disk fully without a bulk eraser (which is a powerful electromagnet).

If the media sensor is not functional, the formatting process is carried out in the high current mode and an 18 sector pattern is created on the disk. This is fine if the disk has the appropriate high coercivity coating but if it is a standard low density disk then the pattern is not easily erasable. As I have already mentioned, this is a major problem with PS/2 models 50, 60, 70 and 80 - earlier PS/2 computers (models 25 and 30) have 720K drives and cannot use 1.44M disks.

The media sensor is standard on all the 1.44M drives I have seen recently but it's action can be disabled or enabled by the computer manufacturer. IBM chose to disable it on the PS/2 range. Thanks, IBM!

The Hard stuff...

Hard disks have been around for several years now and offer a reasonably cost-effective means of storing large amounts of data. Retrieval is usually fast and problem free.

The recording medium in a hard disk consists of one or more aluminium disks (platters), with a magnetic coating on both sides of each disk. The coating is thinner than on floppy disks and data is written to or read from the disks by multiple read/write heads. The spacing between tracks is very small and the need for very accurate positioning of the heads is paramount since there may be several hundred tracks on each platter. The number of sectors per track varies between 17 and about 60, depending upon the type of interface standard which the hard disk supports.

Hard disks must be formatted before they can be used. They normally require two distinct format operations - one, which lays down a physical (or low level) format on the disk, dividing the disk into a series of sectors on each cylinder and filling the data area with a dummy value. After partitioning with FDISK, which sets up one or more spaces in which data can be stored, a logical (high level) format is carried out using the same FORMAT command which is used for floppy disks, although it works differently in this case, and merely sets up the directory and FAT structure. You may recall that the same command, when used for a floppy disk, carries out both a low and high level format. Clever stuff!

The low level format may have been carried out by the manufacturer (and if not, should only be carried out with the correct utility program supplied with the disk). XT-type PCs have a low-level formatting utility built in to the controller and AT-interface (otherwise known as IDE) drives are supplied complete with a low level format and must NOT be low-level formatted by the end user. If you do, then you will ruin the drive which becomes of little more value than a small door stop! Recent computers with AMI BIOS chips can allow the user to carry out this potentially serious operation, with no warning messages. It should only be used with older (non-IDE) drives.

CHAPTER 12
How disk drives work

In the last chapter, the idea of permanent data storage was introduced and some details were given about the way in which data could be stored on disk.

The technology involved in disk operations is relatively simple but extremely precise. It has to be precise in order to ensure that the read/write heads are positioned correctly over the appropriate part of the magnetic medium when required.

Floppy disk drives

The most common sizes of floppy disk drives will take 5.25" and 3.5" disks and the basic principles of drive operation are similar. There are usually two heads and these come in to contact with the upper and lower sides of the disk. A 3.5" drive has a device which slides a protective cover away from the sensitive, exposed area of the disk across which the read/write heads move. In the case of a 5.25" disk, the heads move across a slot cut in the disk cover and the disk is clamped in place onto the drive motor spindle. With the 3.5" disk, locating pegs on the drive motor spindle interlock with holes on the metal centre of the disk and correct, non-slip operation is assured. The location of the read/write head is controlled by a head actuator which is a special type of motor whose spindle rotates in discrete steps, rather than continuously as with the drive motor. It is more correctly known as a stepper motor and coils or uncoils a spring steel band which controls the precise location of the heads which are connected to it. The head assembly slides on low friction guide rails and can move in or out for about 0.5 - 0.75". The stepping rate is 1.8o per track for an 80 track drive and 3.6o for the 40 track type.

The method of data recording on each track has already been dealt with in the last chapter and data tracks are clearly defined and separated by a technique known as tunnel erasing which trims the edges of the data tracks and separates them clearly from the adjacent tracks. The tunnel erasure is designed to produce a specific width of track (0.33 mm for 40 track, 0.16 mm for 80 track 5.25" and 0.115 mm for 3.5" drives). It's worthwhile noting that you should not attempt to format a disk to a density for which it is not designed.

The drive motor is a direct drive type and rotates at 300 r.p.m. in all except 1.2M drives (whose rotational speed is 360 r.p.m.). This is 5 revolutions per second and data is exchanged at a standard rate of 250 KHz in the case of drives intended for 360K and 720K disks. High density 1.44 M drives exchange data at twice this rate (500 KHz). The odd one out is the 360 r.p.m. 1.2 M drive. This spins disks at 360 r.p.m. (6 revolutions per second) and requires a data transmission rate of 500 KHz if high density disks are used or 300 KHz if low density disks are in use. The correct data transmission speed is automatically sensed and all modern floppy disk drive controllers are capable of working at all three data transmission rates (250, 300 and 500 KHz).

The disk drive contains sensors which determine whether or not the disk is write-protected, and high capacity 3.5" drives also check for the presence of high density media so that the data transfer rate can be switched to the lower rate if required - although some drives have this capability removed as in the case of the PS/2 range. All disk drives have an activity light which comes on when the disk is accessed and the disk is either spring ejected (as in 3.5" drives) or clamped/released by opening a flap or pressing a knob and withdrawing the disk manually.

The original low-density 360K drives as fitted to PC-XT computers record 40 tracks initially on one side only but later both side, starting with 0 on the outside edge of the disk. The two heads are labelled as 0 (under-side) and 1 (topside). The drive is usually set up to record 9 sectors per track although some obsolete early disks had 8 sectors per track.

The introduction of the 3.5" 720K drive represented a major step forward in drive technology. This robust disk could be recorded with 80 tracks on both sides and could hold 720K of data with the same 9 sectors per track. Write-protecting against accidental data loss is a matter of sliding a plastic pad from one position to another.

The 720K drive was fitted to a wide range of XT and AT type computers and could be used with the same disk controller as was used for the original low density 360K drive as long as the BIOS (a chip which contains the basic instructions to allow the computer to communicate with the outside world) is able to support it. In practice, this means that all except early IBM and clone XT systems (before mid-1985) are suitable, and it is possible to get replacement floppy disk controller cards which will enable the system to cope with modern drives and media.

As developments proceeded. the capacity of the 3.5" drive was doubled by the adoption of a higher rate of data transfer and high coercivity disks in 1987. As with the low density 720K disk, there are 80 tracks on each side but the number of sectors was doubled to 18. Track 0 is on the outside and the last track (79) on the inside. Since the 720K disk does not have a high density media sensing hole in its case, the data transfer rate is automatically set to 250 KHz, rather than 500 KHz required by the higher density types. The recent introduction of the 2.88M disk involves increasing the number of sectors to 36, and will necessitate a data transfer rate of 1MHz. Only the most recent floppy disk controllers will be able to cope with this very high transfer rate and most system users will stick with the 500KHz transfer rate until the prices of the new controllers and the high capacity disks fall to a sensible level.

The 5.25" high density 1.2 M floppy disk drive was introduced in 1984 in the IBM AT system. It was designed to use a high coercivity 80 track double-sided disk, divided into 15 sectors per track and to be downwards-compatible with the earlier 360K low density disk. The degree of compatibility was not complete and problems exists with reading and writing to the 360K disk.

The drive was designed to be able to imitate a 40 track drive by double-stepping the heads, effectively missing out every other track. The read/write head is used to write a narrower track (0.16 mm) than in a 360K drive, and cannot over-write the full track width (0.33 mm) of a 40 track disk formatted in a low density drive. Accordingly, some of the original recording is left and if the disk is then read in a standard 360K drive, the system may well be seriously confused by picking up both the original and the new data which is embedded within it!

The only way in which low density disks can be reliably written or read in a 1.2M drive is for a brand new or magnetically erased disk to be formatted to 360K using the /4 or /f:360 option. The disk can then be written to in the 1.2M drive and the files will be perfectly intelligible to a 360K drive.

Hard Disks

The technology underlying the design and operation of most hard disks is quite similar to that of the floppy disk drive. Apart from the larger capacity and the fact that most hard disks cannot be taken out of the machine (one or two manufacturers have experimented with this idea), the similarities outweigh the differences.

Early hard disks as used in PCs had quite small capacities (5 or 10 M was quite common) while current drives have capacities in excess of 1 Gigabyte (1000 megabytes). The early hard disks were 5.25" in size, and Full Height (about 3" tall); newer drives are half this height and an increasing number of 3.5" types are built to a standard or slim-line specification. Even smaller drives (2") are available but are still quite expensive.

Hard disks often have several magnetically-coated rigid disks (platters) and each platter has two read/write heads moving very closely over the surface. The platters are spun by a powerful, constant speed motor (usually 3600 r.p.m.) and the heads are fixed together on a bracket and are usually actuated by a solenoid or stepper motor so that they move in and out between the platters in a precisely controlled fashion.

The platters, heads and head positioning mechanism are contained within a sealed container known as the head/disk assembly (HDA) which has been assembled under virtually dust-free conditions in a specially designed 'clean room'. The HDA must not be opened or otherwise interfered with since even the smallest particle of dust may cause damage to the magnetic surface of a platter if it becomes trapped between the head and the platter. More fundamental damage can be caused by physical shock such as knocking the disk when it is in use. This can cause a head-crash to occur, where the read/write heads which float about 0.00003 - 0.0001 mm on a cushion of air just above the platter surface hit the platter and damage the magnetic coating and any data thereon. The same effect can be caused by larger dust particles - hence the warning about opening an HDA in your workshop.

The platter is usually made of aluminium alloy - very occasionally of glass and each is about 3 mm thick. The magnetic coating (medium) is one of two types - either oxide-based or the more recently developed thin film. Early types of hard disk used the oxide medium which was made from a finely dispersed iron oxide slurry which was spread on the spinning platters and produced a thin, even coating about 0.00008 mm in thickness. The film is hardened and polished before use and can hold up to 20,000 magnetic flux changes per track inch. The drawback with oxide coatings is their fragility and consequent prone-ness to head crash damage. It has also been reported that the medium has a tendency to flake off following a head crash.

The more recent type of medium is known as a thin film since the deposition process plates or sputters a series of very thin (0.000008 mm) coatings including a layer of a cobalt/iron oxide mixture which is the recording medium. Plating, as it's name suggests is an electrical method in which the platters are immersed in a series of solutions which deposit the layers electrochemically. Sputtering is a vastly different process in which the platters are coated in near-vacuum conditions and the end result is a hard-wearing ultra-smooth magnetic coating which will be less susceptible to head crashes than oxide-coated platters. The plating process is also quite satisfactory but the final quality of finish is not as good as sputtering will produce. It must be said that sputtered disks are more expensive to produce, but are increasingly used in high capacity systems since the medium can hold over 50,000 magnetic flux changes per track inch.

The point has been made that oxide-coated surfaces are more fragile than sputtered or plated surfaces and this is of importance in the event of a head crash. The head crash occurs when a read/write head comes into contact with the spinning disk platter. On an oxide-coated surface, the head may well score a groove in the surface and the resultant damage may totally or partially destroy any data that was there and there may be problems in writing to that area. A further complication is that some of the ploughed material may cause other head crashes because of it's size. The thinner coating on a plated or sputtered disk is also harder and the head may well bounce off without causing any significant damage - although the head itself may be knocked about. Any part of the disk which is damaged in this way, so that it will not reliably hold data, is referred to as a bad sector.

Heads

Each platter has 2 read/write heads associated with it - one on each side. In the simplest system, a hard disk will have one platter and 2 heads but there could be up to 11 platters (22 read/write heads) in some high capacity systems. The heads are mounted on a spring-loaded pivoted arm whose position is accurately controlled either by a 'stepper motor actuator' (or SMA) (as in a floppy drive) or by a specialised solenoid called a 'voice-coil actuator' (or VCA). The heads move in and out between the spinning platters. The performance of an SMA, when moving between tracks, is about 40 - 60 ms per track, compared with about 15 - 30 ms for the VCA drives.

Originally, the read/write heads were made from a composite ferrite material and were not unlike very small versions of the tape heads used in cassette players. These are relatively bulky but cheap to make and were favoured for low cost designs. Their greater mass made them more subject to head crash damage and they could not write to such high densities on plated or sputtered media.

Modern drives tend to use thin-film heads which are made from a semi-conductor material and are much lighter and able to spin closer to the disk surface. This means that the amount of signal that can be retrieved is improved and the signal to noise (S/N) ratio of the head/medium combination is high enough to allow very dense data packing on each cylinder. Another feature of the thin film head is that a greater signal amplitude can be recorded on the disk and this will also contribute to a high S/N ratio and greater accuracy of recording. All magnetic media have background noise - the amount of which depends upon the composition of the medium. Iron oxide media are noisier (more perceptible 'hiss') than cobalt or chrome types, a feature which will be familiar to users of audio cassette tape. With digital systems, such as are used in data recording, the S/N ratio isn't as important as it would be in high quality sound recording, but under some circumstances, it is possible to lose a digital signal in amongst the background noise. This is another reason why neither oxide media nor composite heads are not found in high capacity drives.

Hard and soft errors

The chances of a drive remaining totally trouble-free are fairly good, provided that it is well looked after. On the other hand, damage may occur which will not necessarily stop it dead but which will cause intermittent data errors. Sometimes this damage may result from a hardware malfunction, such as a head crash which wipes out part of a track - and any attempt on the part of the system to read data from or write data to that track will fail. This sort of problem is called a hard error since it will not go away!

Soft errors occur less predictably - even when the system works correctly, but there is often no pattern to their occurrence. Typically, a power surge may trigger such an event, although failing drive mechanisms can also cause soft errors, the number and regularity of which increases as the point of failure nears! The drive controller can often cope with soft errors since it tries to read or write the data up to 10 times before chickening out and informing your operating system of the problem. DOS will then have another try, prior to referring the matter back to the controller. DOS has up to 3 attempts at reading or writing until it gives up with an appropriate error message. The problem must be quite intractable if 30 separate attempts are made. Soft errors are probably more common than one might imagine and it's only the worst cases that come to our notice through a screen message.

Error correction

Error detection and correction are carried out by hard disk controllers which calculate a CRC (cyclic redundancy code) from blocks of data which are then written immediately after the data in each sector. When the data is read again, another CRC is calculated and compared with the stored value. If the codes do not correspond, an error must have occurred and correction will then take place, if at all possible. The recovery process may involve re-reading the disk.

Stepper vs. voice coil

The mechanism that controls the movement of the read/write heads across the platters is precisely controlled by a head actuator. These are known as stepper motor actuators or voice coil actuators; the former type are found in older low cost, low capacity drives while larger capacity drives tend to have the latter. In terms of reliability, the voice coil actuator is superior in almost every way to the stepper motor type. This is because the VCA is neither temperature- nor positionally-sensitive, access times are faster and the heads are designed to park out of the way when not required.

Stepper motors work well with floppy drives which have a maximum track density of 135 tracks per inch for 3.5" and 96 for 5.25" 80 track. Most hard disks have greater track densities than the figure quoted for a 3.5" drive, and the need for very accurate positioning is apparent, so that mis-tracking can be avoided. Unfortunately, disk drives tend to be mounted inside cabinets which allow then to get quite hot, even when running normally. Aluminium platters expand and contract as they heat up and cool down and in doing so, may get out of alignment with the stepper motor. The stepper motor will only allow the head to move in increments of 1 step and this may not be enough to correct the temperature-induced problem where the track may have expanded or contracted by a fraction of a step. VCA control automatically compensates for temperature changes.

When disks are initially formatted, the general rule is to attempt to carry out the formatting at the working temperature of the disk - so a hard disk can be mounted in a computer and allowed to reach it's working temperature before the low level format is carried out. Once formatted, the tracks and sectors will be correct for that temperature, but there is a possibility of problems when the disk first starts up since the data may well be written to one side of the formatted track and could even be missed altogether when the disk is warm. This is not a pleasant state of affairs and happened quite often with hard cards (a 3.5" hard drive and controller card mounted on a plate which would plug into one of the expansion slots on the computer mother board). The cards that were most often affected were formatted using a Run Length Limited (RLL) data encoding which packed 50% more data on a given disk compared with the standard MFM (Modified Frequency Modulation) encoding.

Thankfully, these types of disk drives are less often met with now and the attendant data errors and other problems are very rarely encountered. If you have one of these drives and you encounter data errors, then the most sensible way of tackling it is to backup all your data and carry out a complete low level and high level format before restoring the data to the disk. If you want to, it is possible to use one of the commercially available or public domain programs that enable the re-format to go ahead without saving data. In this case, the program copies the data from a track to a spare location elsewhere on the disk and then re-formats the original track prior to replacing the data. It's quite a sensible way of doing things but if you have a power cut during the process, this can cause major problems since data may be lost. That's why all such programs advise you to make a backup before you use them. Typical programs are Bracking's HDTEST, Disk Technician Gold and Gibson Research's SPINRITE - the last two also check your disk very thoroughly for bad sectors and generally investigate how the controller and disk are performing.

The voice coil actuator works like an electromagnet. Current is passed through the coil (which surrounds a magnet) and this causes the coil and head assembly to move in or out. The head assembly is provided with a light spring which pulls the heads back to a 'landing zone', usually on a track where no data is recorded, when the power to a VCA drive is switched off. This is known as self-parking and is a feature not normally met with in stepper-actuated head assemblies. One or two drive types actually retract the heads into a cage away from the disks where no harm can be caused.

The VCA system is fast and accurate since the heads can be stopped anywhere over the platter surface. Accordingly some form of track marking must be provided and this is normally done by taking one side of one platter (known as a dedicated servo surface) out of normal use and recording on it a set of index marks which determine the positions of the tracks. One of the heads (known as the servo-controlled index head) scans this information and the electronics work out which track a particular index refers to. Once the head is moved to that position (which occurs very rapidly), the head assembly stops moving apart from a slight adjustment to give the strongest signal. The system is neat and very reliable.

At one time, most VCA drives were identifiable because they had an odd number of read/write heads (my old faithful CDC 40-odd Mbyte drive has 5 heads) but more advanced designs have the servo-information embedded in the sector gaps for each track and this avoids the need for a dedicated surface. In these cases, there is normally an even number of heads.

Earthing problems

Some manufacturers mount their hard disks on plastic slides for ease of installation. This can sometimes cause problems with data owing to earthing problems - the metal chassis of the drive should be electrically connected to the metalwork of the case. This is usually carried out using screws but where slides are used, the drive may be insulated. Even small amounts of electrical noise or differences in electric potential can cause problems with data transmission but the cure is very simple - usually a wire connected between the frame of the drive onto a nearby portion of the case. Some drives have metal tags which take Lucar (slide-on) connectors and by which they can be 'earthed'.

CHAPTER 13
Floppy disk problems

Floppy disks are surprisingly robust - yet, under the right (or rather, the wrong) conditions, data can be lost or data storage problems can develop.

Most floppy disk problems are due either to careless handling, to the use of an inappropriate disk type, or to incorrect use of copying or formatting commands.   Modern floppy disk drives are exceedingly reliable but if they go wrong, it's best to buy a new drive, rather than try to get the old one repaired.

Let's look at the handling problems - dirty fingers, leaving a 5.25" disk out of it's envelope, smoking near the computer or disks, putting it near a hot surface or a magnetic field.   Each of these can cause loss of data over part or the whole of the disk, and this will almost certainly mean that you will have to use one of the commercial packages such as PC Tools or Norton to attempt to get the data back.

Wrong disk types account for a few problems.   Usually, someone decides that they want to save a bit of money and they format a double density 3.5" disk to high density standard.   This usually works and doubles the capacity of the disk - but the type of magnetic medium used on 720K disks will not retain the high density format and data retention after a month or two is pretty poor.

If you try the same trick with double density 5.25" disks, the attempt to format them to 1.2Mbytes will probably yield a disk with several hundred thousand bytes in bad sectors!   Some users have managed, against all odds, to format a high density 5.25" disk in an Amstrad PC low density disk drive.   A friend of mine did this and was able to use the disk for a while, until it gave a final 'General failure error' message and died, with no possibility of resuscitation.

Wrong use of commands probably causes more hassle than anything else.

If you FORMAT a floppy disk - or a hard disk for that matter, you will lose all the data on the disk. If you have DOS 5 or 6 installed in your system, it may be possible to recover the data after an inadvertent format, otherwise, you will have lost it for good.

Copying disks can be dangerous if you use the DISKCOPY command without thinking. This is easy to do because copying lots of floppy disks is excessively boring. DISKCOPY only allows you to copy from and to disks of the same size and media - so you cannot copy a 3.5" high density on to a 3.5" double density disk. Copying with this command means that you have to swap the source disk and the target disk when prompted - could be three or four times if the disks are high density types.

The source disk and destination disks should be labelled before you start, because it's very easy to get them mixed up. If you get it wrong, you may well have lost everything. Now, I always set the write-protect tab on my source disks after one awful experience when I thought I'd lost some irreplaceable files - the thought of re-typing a whole thesis concentrates the mind wonderfully!

Disk errors

A lot of disk errors can be avoided by regular maintenance. The DOS CHKDSK utility is quite a powerful tool in it's own right, particularly if used regularly. Normally, you would just type:

```
CHKDSK A:
```

This will report if there are problems, but it will not attempt to fix them for you.

If, having used CHKDSK without any parameters, you want to look at the state of a disk, simply type:

```
CHKDSK A:
```

This will check through the disk in drive A, and reports if it finds any problem.

```
CHKDSK A: /F
```

can be used as well. The /F switch or parameter instructs CHKDSK to 'fix' the problem but should be used with great care if any files are reported as being cross-linked.

Any disk will accumulate what are known as 'lost clusters' which occur when a program finishes incorrectly, or when a machine is re-booted because it appears to have 'hung'. The /F switch can be very helpful because it converts lost clusters to files which can be examined and deleted if they are of no use - that goes for most such files. Any files which are not needed will take up valuable disk space, so they should be erased.

Operating problems

Power failures

If the power supply is interrupted while your PC is accessing a disk, this can cause all manner of mayhem, so try to avoid this sort of situation if at all possible.

It may be very difficult to recover data from disks which have suffered in this way, and this is why so many commercial organisations have Uninterruptible Power Supply (UPS) systems which will take over in a fraction of a second if the mains power fails. Domestic users shouldn't need to worry about installing a UPS unless their mains supply is of very poor quality. Electrical 'spikes' can have a similar effect; the best cure for the latter problem is the purchase of a surge-limiting plug.

Disk removal

Taking a disk out of a drive when it is being written to by a program will lead to confusion on the part of the program and computer and also to data loss through scrambling.

Disk fragmentation.

This is more of a problem with hard disks but can also occur with higher capacity floppies. Essentially, fragmentation means that the the disk has been well used and many files are erased, written, erased and written until any free space on the disk is fragmented into small patches. Defragmentation re-organises free space and the data so that files are not broken up into small chunks and spread out all over the place. Commercial programs like Norton and PC Tools will do this for you; the de-fragmentation utility in DOS 6 only works with hard disks. Fragmentation is responsible for slowing down the response of hard disks, and some writers recommend defragmenting once a month or so. I do it about 3 or 4 times a year.

Disk capacity

One problem that many users seem to encounter quite a lot, is when they are saving files to a floppy disk after working on them, particularly with word-processor programs. These programs backup whatever they are working with, either automatically or manually and when the files get big, there may be insufficient space to accommodate the edited file and it's backup. It is usually possible to delete files but if not, you may be able to insert a fresh disk instead. It's never a good idea to work with very large document files on floppies. I would advise you to keep the file size below 30K which is equivalent to about 4,500 words of text.

Cheap disks

Disk prices are pretty low at present, even for branded types, and it doesn't make sense to use second-quality disks if it can be avoided. Branded types are normally very reliable and most have lifetime guarantees which means that you should keep your receipts or invoices for a year or two, just in case a replacement is required. Unbranded disks are probably as good but probably won't have the stylish packing or pretty disk labels. I tend to buy these because I find them reliable.

'Seconds' may be OK, but in my experience, I have found problems with data retention, stability of the magnetic coating and dirt. Some 3.5" disks had jammed data shutters while others had no write-protect slider.

Several firms offer disks at low prices and they are pretty reliable. There is no point in paying 'over the odds' for posh branded disks, so check prices carefully and see if there are any extras such as disk boxes which you don't want.

CHAPTER 14
Hard disk interfaces and Interleave

A hard disk, even when supplied with power, isn't a lot of use unless it can be connected to your system in a manner that will allow it to exchange data in a reasonably civilised fashion. This is normally achieved by means of a controller, which can translate the signals passing between the disk and the system. This type of controller is sometimes referred to as an interface and will conform (to a greater or lesser extent) to one of four specifications - ST506 or ST412, ESDI, SCSI and IDE.

The four basic types of hard disk interface which are found in PCs have widely differing characteristics.

ST 506/412

Older disk drives use the Seagate ST506 interface which was designed to accommodate their 5 Mbyte drives and subsequently used by many other manufacturers. A year or so later, Seagate introduced an improved version (ST412) which has a buffered seek capability to improve the performance of the system. Because of the dual origin of the standard, it is widely known as the ST506/412.

The maximum capacity of any drive which can be given this interface is 150Mbytes in MFM or 230 Mbytes in RLL mode. The MFM standard uses 17 sectors per track and RLL increases this to 26, but the rate of data transfer is quite slow, compared with other types of interface. The maximum rate at which data transfer can take place depends upon the interleave factor - normally between 1:3 and 1:1 - and the encoding scheme.

With MFM, the maximum rate of data transfer is about 500 Kbytes/sec., and about 900 Kbytes/sec. in RLL mode. RLL does suffer from problems with reliability on oxide media owing to the higher density of the magnetic domains but modern plated coatings and high quality electronics seem to indicate that RLL encoding is still a viable proposition.

In order to use an ST506/412 drive in a system, the details of the disk may have to be entered prior to a low level format (for XT systems) or entered into the drive tables in an AT system.   The XT option tends to restrict the number of drive types which can be used and the AT option is a little easier in that modern clone BIOSes such as AMI allow you to specify the exact parameters of your disk.   It's important to note that the setting up of the disk in an XT system may be less than ideal. This is because the XT controller BIOS was not designed to cope with the large number of drive types and parameters available today. The same is true of early IBM AT machines and their clones.

ESDI

The ESDI standard can be used for hard disks and tape drives and is capable of extremely high rates of data transfer as well as being intrinsically more reliable than the earlier ST412 interface on which it is based.   The specified maximum data transfer is 3 Mbytes /sec. but current drives are limited to rather lower transfer rates at present - up to 1.25 or 2 Mbytes /sec.

ESDI Drives can have 32 or more sectors per track and some have 50 and more; in consequence, ESDI drives offer high capacity. Apart from the speed of data transfer, the ESDI standard allows the drive controller to read details of bad sectors and drive geometry from the drive itself, thus overcoming the need to enter these details manually.

ESDI controllers are able to offer 1:1 interleave which permits a 1Mbyte/sec. or greater data transfer rate, compared with 500 Kbytes/sec. on an MFM encoded ST506/412.

ESDI is the current IBM standard interface for PS/2 systems with 70 Mbyte or greater capacity hard disks and in general, ESDI and ST506/412 interfaces are compatible. This is not the case with the next interface - the SCSI.

SCSI

The SCSI ('scuzzy') interface operates in a different manner from the types of interface already described. It is deigned to operate at the systems level and the interface allows the user to plug in other controllers and allow them to communicate with each other. SCSI allows you to use ESDI or ST506/412 drives and controllers which will plug into the SCSI interface. The system is designed to allow up to 8 controllers into the interface and allow one to act as a host and control access to the system from the computer's data bus.

Many different types of equipment can be connected via the SCSI - such as scanners, CD 'ROM players and tape streamers. SCSI hard drives have a controller and SCSI attachment built in and cannot be 'daisy-chained' like ESDI, IDE and ST506/412 types - instead, up to 7 can be attached to one host adapter. The manner in which drives and attachments are developing indicates that for most purposes, SCSI is the preferred choice for systems expansion. This is fair enough in principle but depends for it's success on an agreed standard which, unfortunately, does not yet exist. Some manufacturers' products aren't fully compatible with the standard which is, admittedly, rather imprecise in it's drafting.

A new standard - SCSI II - does exist and is being phased in to cope with some of the current problems. Some problems exist because there is no host adapter standard, software interface or hard disk ROM BIOS support for drives attached to this bus. The matter is being addressed - and not before time - by a limited number of companies, including IBM who released the first SCSI adapters, peripherals and ROM BIOS support for the PS/2 system.

IDE (sometimes referred to as the AT interface)

IDE drives were originally designed to be plugged into an expansion slot and contained a built-in disk controller. The reason for doing this as to reduce the chances of installation problems and to reduce the lengths of cable carrying high frequency signals which might contribute to reliability problems.

Now, IDE drives tend to be mounted together with the floppy drives in a more secure environment and a cable connects the drive to the motherboard. Some motherboards do not have an IDE connector and these require the drive to plug into an adapter which plugs into the expansion bus sockets. Certain types of cards have a buffering capability which allows the system to take advantage of the speed of the interface. The buffer allows more information to be read than is actually needed and this may help when the next request to read data is issued - the data is already available in memory. This simple process can improve the rate of data transfer quite a lot.

There are three types of IDE interface - each specific to a particular data bus. The PS/2 range of computers (starting with the model 50) have an MCA (micro-channel architecture) version which has a 72 pin connector. AT systems have a 16-bit controller and XT systems have an 8-bit controller, both with a 40 pin connector. The XT and AT types are not interchangeable, but the former type isn't particularly common.

The IDE drive is currently very popular because of it's reliability and good performance but appears at present to be limited to drives with a capacity less than about 350 Mbytes.

A couple of technical terms need to be defined as far as IDE drives are concerned. The physical geometry of the drive (number of read/write heads, cylinders and sectors) is referred to as the Native mode (which is the same for all other types of hard disk). The normal operating mode is referred to as the Translation mode in which the drive will support any disk geometry provided the following conditions are met:

Number of read/write heads is 16 or less

Number of logical cylinders is 1024 or less

The resulting number of sectors does not exceed the guaranteed number of sectors on the disk.

To take an example - my Seagate ST157A guarantees me 87360 sectors and has a native mode geometry of 6 read/write heads, 26 sectors per track and 560 tracks (multiply these figures together to get the guaranteed number of sectors). In translation mode, I can set it up as a 733 track, 17 sector and 7 head device which enables me to use all but about 130 sectors. You should not attempt to use an IDE drive in it's native mode. The encoding method for IDE is a form of RLL and the drive is 'intelligent' when compared with drives operating with the ST506/412 interface.

Apart from the power connector (which usually supplies 12 and 5 volts to the drives) the ST506/412 and ESDI types have a couple of flat cables - a 34 way control cable and a 20 way data cable and the SCSI normally uses a single 50 way cable.

Interleave

This is a term used to describe the pattern in which data is written to a hard disk. The interleave factor of modern drives and AT or PS/2 controller combinations is 1:1 which means that the disk will accept data as fast as the controller can transfer it - similarly, the controller can take data from the disk very rapidly.

Older disk controllers and disk drives were not so sprightly and could not read consecutive sectors from one revolution of the hard disk. To take a simple example - if each track of the hard disk was divided into 17 sectors, a 1:1 interleave means that the controller reads or write sectors 1,2,3....17 in sequence.

The disk is rotating at 3600 r.p.m. so 1 revolution of the disk occurs in 1/60th of a second (0.01667 sec.) and a sector will pass the read/write heads every 1/17 x 60 or 0.0098 sec.. On this basis, a complete sector would need to be read or written in 10 milliseconds.....

Older controllers and disks, particularly those used in XT machines could not cope with this rate of data transfer and would miss data, and it was found that setting the system so that the heads read every other or every third sector would overcome the problem. In some extreme cases, the interleave had to be fixed at 7:1 which meant that the disk had to revolve 7 times for all the data to be read or written.

The following diagram should make this clear:

Sector numbers accessed

interleave

1:1 - 1	2	3	4	5	6	7	8	9	10	11	12	13	14	15	16	17
2:1 - 1	10	2	11	3	12	4	13	5	14	6	15	7	16	8	17	9
3:1 - 1	7	13	2	8	14	3	9	15	4	10	16	5	11	17	6	12
4:1 - 1	14	10	6	2	15	11	7	3	16	12	8	4	17	13	9	5
5:1 - 1	8	15	5	12	2	9	16	6	13	3	10	17	7	14	4	11
6:1 - 1	4	7	10	13	16	2	5	8	11	14	17	3	6	7	12	15
7:1 - 1	6	11	16	4	9	14	2	7	12	17	5	10	15	3	8	13

With the development of faster controllers for AT machines, it was possible to use most ST506/412 interface drives at an interleave of 3:1 or 2:1, or in some cases 1:1 if the controller was up to it. The problems which arose if either a slow drive and fast controller (or vice-versa) were matched and set up with a 1:1 interleave was one of data loss or corruption and could only be solved if a slower transfer rate (greater interleave) was used. The standard ST506 interface could handle 500Kbytes /sec. at a 1:1 interleave with MFM encoding but if the 1:1 interleave was incorrect for the drive/controller combination, this could mean that it would take up to 17 revolutions to read a full track which gives a data transfer rate of 30 Kbytes/sec. which is pretty dreadful. The situation with RLL encoding and interleave is similar, apart from the fact that there are 26 sectors per track. ESDI, SCSI and IDE drives almost always work with an interleave of 1:1 and data transfer rates are optimised.

CHAPTER 15
Care and management of hard disks

In any computer system, the most vulnerable part is the hard disk. Floppy disk drives are less vulnerable because the magnetic medium (the floppy disk) can be removed, whereas with most hard disks, the magnetic medium remains in the machine at all times.

In an earlier chapter, we saw how a hard disk was constructed, and how data is recorded on the disk surfaces. In this chapter, we will see how it is possible to maintain your hard drive so that most potential sources of disaster are avoided.

DOS (prior to the introduction of MSDOS 5) provided no easily usable tools to help with disk care and maintenance, and as a result, a number of authors have devised programs or packages which do most of the things that are required to help the user sleep easily at night! Some of these programs are available as Shareware (try before you buy) while others are reasonably inexpensive, if you consider what they can do for you.

Problems

A hard disk contains several mechanical parts such as a number of flat disks, usually revolving at about 3600 r.p.m., and, moving just above the disk surface, the red/write heads. There is considerable potential for mechanical trouble here and the likely frequency of problems will increase with the age of the disk drive.

It is always better to locate the source of problems before they become serious enough to affect the data stored on the disk, and a regular backup of hard disk files is essential if you are to avoid disaster. There are facilities within DOS to do this, or you can use one of the shareware or commercial programs - but, in any case, just do it regularly!

There are five basic types of errors to which hard drives are prone:

Hard errors

These are errors caused by a physical problem with the recording surface which cases incorrect or corrupt data to be read from the disk. Hard errors cannot be put right easily since the structure of the recording surface has a flaw. Instead, the area should be marked as unusable so that data will not be stored there in future.

Soft errors

These occur when corrupted data is found on the disk, but unlike hard errors, soft errors can be overcome by re-writing the corrupted area with correct data. The problem causes a lot of difficulty if the offending area is on the first couple of cylinders of the disk since this is where a lot of the system and file information is kept. Data loss through soft errors is quite common, and is another good reason for backing up on a regular basis.

Logical errors

These happen when problems are encountered with the file allocation table (FATs) and directories that DOS uses to keep tack of files. The CHKDSK program in DOS will show up some logical errors, usually in the form of 'lost clusters' if the disk has them. A lost cluster is one that is marked as being in use by a file, but not actually allocated to any of the files on the disk. Logical errors can occur as a result of power-line surges, changing disks while data is being written (only with floppies) or as a result of unfriendly programs which crash or stop working (hang up) while writing information to the disk. The FATs and directory can become totally confused - definitely unpleasant. If you are using compressed disks, then you may encounter logical errors on both the compressed drives and host drives - even nastier!

Alignment errors

This type of error is mechanical in origin and alignment errors tend to get worse with the age of the disk. They are a particular problem with older MFM and, particularly RLL drives which use stepper motors to position the read/write heads, but they can also arise as a result of an accumulation of very small changes in the alignment of the disk drive heads relative to the media. This sometimes results in areas of the disk being unreadable since the head position is no longer correct. Data loss can be avoided by using fairly sophisticated adjustment programs, but the best cure is to take off as much data as possible and then to re-format the disk.

Intermittent errors

Sometimes, the sort of errors that occur may do so on an irregular basis - the classic case as far as hard disks are concerned is when a sector on the disk surface has a flaw which is only marginally faulty. The data recorded on it can be read on many occasions without trouble, but just once in a while, it cannot. Usually this sort of problem can be overcome by re-trying the operation a couple of times.

Preventative maintenance

If a hard disk drive has been in use for several months, or even a year or two, it is a wise policy to 'spring clean' or service it. This will sort out many of the actual problems you may encounter - such as soft errors, and may also deal with hidden errors such as those which occur intermittently, or faulty media problems. If you buy a second-hand disk, give it the same treatment! As was pointed out earlier, magnetic patterns aren't permanent and fade over a period of time. It is therefore important to refresh the recorded data and to check that it is valid.

The Boot disk

Before carrying out any maintenance, make sure that you have a Boot floppy disk. This will have an operating system with the relevant files, together with any additional information to get the system up and running. Both PC Tools and Norton Utilities give you the option of making a Recovery Disk when you first install them and this will take care of the problem. Do remember to include any special drivers your system needs if, for example, Disk Manager or disk compression programs have been used. If these are not loaded as DEVICES in the CONFIG.SYS file, the system will not function correctly and you may not be able to access the hard disk. This boot disk can be created by using the following command from DOS:

```
FORMAT A: /s /v
```

This carries out both a low- and high-level format on the floppy disk, and puts an operating system and the three basic files that it needs. Don't forget to write a little CONFIG.SYS file to hold the files=20 and buffers=30 parameters as well as any essential device drivers. Avoid loading files from the AUTOEXEC.BAT program unless they're really necessary, and then write-protect the disk to avoid the possibility of Virus infection.

I always run the DOS CHKDSK program whenever I am about to tidy up a hard disk.

This because CHKDSK investigates the organisation of the disk and how consistent it is, since the action of creating a file on a disk not only creates a directory entry (which you can see when you type DIR at the command prompt), but also allocates space for the file on the disk by putting special markers in the File Allocation Table (FAT). CHKDSK compares the FAT information with the directory structure and warns if there are any discrepancies. In this case, it will usually report that that there are a 'number of lost clusters in a number of chains' or, in more severe cases, it will mention 'cross linked chains'. If there are any lost clusters, it will ask if it may convert them into a file. If you type 'N' in response, it ignores the lost clusters, but if you weaken and type 'Y', then it places them in the excitingly-named FILENNNN.CHK on the disk you've tested (the NNNN is a series number from 0001 to 9999). Have a look at the contents of these files, and delete them if they are gibberish - which 90% are! It is sometimes possible to extract some valuable information from these .CHK files, but don't rely on it. Most problems of this sort are caused by programs which become confused, thus causing your computer to hang - and when the only way to interrupt is to re-boot the computer. This process stops the problem but prevents the program from tidying up after itself.

CHKDSK can also be run with one or both of two optional parameters. Be very careful, though!

CHKDSK C: /V will list all the files on disk C and tell you if they are fragmented. CHKDSK C: /V /F is potentially dangerous since it will attempt to fix anything that it considers to be wrong - and not all of it's fixes are correct!

If I need to do some work on a disk, I boot up the system from a floppy disk (as mentioned earlier in this chapter) rather than from the hard disk. This eliminates problems which might be caused by program conflicts.

What next?

There's a lot of software around which promises to do all that you want. Some is good and you take your disk's life in your hands if you use others.

I happen to like a Shareware program called **HDTEST**, by Jim

Bracking. It's reliable and does a good job in almost all cases, allowing you to adjust the interleave, surface scan the disk, carry out a non-destructive low-level format and all manner of other tests and tweaks. There's a lot more good shareware disk utilities around.

I also like Gibson Research's **Spinrite** program - this carries out some very rigorous testing and it can be used in batch or interactive mode. Some people reckon that it's not safe to use, but, provided you read the manual carefully before running it, you should be OK. I've used Spinrite for several years now and haven't (fingers crossed) had a problem with it.

Spinrite can low-level format your disk. This may be useful with older MFM or RLL disks but you must not do this to modern IDE drives, so it is as well to turn off this feature.

As part of it's testing, Spinrite checks the rotational speed of the disk, and determines the interleave. This may be useful for older drives, but it is irrelevant as far as newer drive and controller types are concerned since they normally work with a 1:1 interleave. It also checks the positioning of the read/write heads so that they can be placed with absolute certainty over the correct track band the reliability of this is dependent on the head positioning mechanism - be it voice coil or stepper motor. It does this for the complete drive and can take a long time on a slow drive. This feature can be turned off if required.

Normally, you will want to test the media and SPINRITE allows you to carry out a quick scan which reads the disk and will pick up major problems without a detailed test. Otherwise, you can opt for much more rigorous testing. Spinrite tests every part of the magnetic media with five patterns of data and shifted variations of these. You can carry this out with 5 repetitions - which does little more than test the read/write circuitry and other aspects of the drive and it's controller, and only picks up the more serious defects. The next most severe test has 43 repetitions of the pattern test and will catch most, but not all defects. The ultimate test is 82 repetitions and this catches all surface defects.

If they are recoverable, it does just this and returns the sectors and clusters with which they are associated, to active use but only if you specify this option.

The depth of pattern testing and the capacity of the drive will influence the time the whole procedure takes. A high capacity drive on the most detailed testing could well take several days or more of continuous running to process - and you may not be able to spare the machine for that length of time. Spinrite allows you to suspend the operations and allows you return to them later on to finish the test. Once started, it will, after a short while, give you a realistic estimate of the time needed to complete the tests.

There are a number of other commercial programs which can be used to test the integrity of your hard disk. I happen to like Norton Utilities and PC Tools, but mostly, I use Norton's programs because I have a copy on my PC at home. I have PC Tools on my machine at work, so there's no favouritism!

Let's look at the relevant facilities offered by each.

Norton Utilities is currently at version 7 and offers the following:

Disk Doctor - which analyses and tests the organisation of those high-level disk structures which MSDOS (or PCDOS) uses for data storage. In particular, it checks the FAT, Boot sector, partition table and the directory tree structure for errors and anomalous material of both hard and floppy disks. It also tests the integrity of all data clusters on the disk and, where possible, corrects any errors it encounters while checking the disk. Versions earlier than 7.0 could not analyse and deal with problems associated with the use of Stacker, Superstor or Doublespace disk compression.

Calibrate operates at a low level - below that of the format used prior to data transfer - and carries out detailed tests and analysis of the low-level structures on the disk which support DOS file operations. In this respect, it is remarkably similar in it's mode of action to Spinrite. Formatting a disk involves two operations - the initial low-level format to establish the basic data structure - effectively a three level hierarchy of disk sides, tracks (sometimes known as cylinders) and sectors. The low level format also writes sector header information on the disk which provides information needed by the disk controller. The high level format prepares the data structure already present and leaves it ready for use. Calibrate only works with hard disks, and in common with Disk Doctor, it will not work with network or purely logical drives.

I use the Calibrate program as a means of checking and refreshing the data on drives which might be a little suspect. It carries out these processes without destroying or disturbing the data in any way and can be invaluable where intermittent read errors have begun to occur. It will also sort out the majority of hard and soft errors.

Another feature of Calibrate is it's ability to adjust the sector interleave, so that drives which are less than optimally configured can be persuaded to deliver a much better data transfer performance. This feature is normally only of use with older types of drive.

My only serious reservation about Calibrate is its lack of a 'Resume' function during pattern testing.

Calibrate and Norton Disk Doctor can handle most disk problems but from time to time, the versatility of Disk Editor as a recovery tool may come in handy.

Disk Editor is able to access any part of a hard or floppy disk and can be used to inspect data on disks which have damage top the root directory or partition table. It enables you to carry out remedial action by writing new information directly to particular parts of the disk, and it also allows you to copy information from the faulty disk and transfer this to an undamaged disk or even to a safe part of the same disk. Data recovery by this method can take a long time and complete success cannot be guaranteed.

Disk Editor can access both the system and data areas of a disk without any major difficulty, regardless of the state of the data on the disk. It cannot easily cope with disks which are physically damaged by folding, crumpling or having been used as pincushions. It uses two modes of access - logical and physical. The logical approach is the default.

In logical mode, Disk Editor operates by using the standard structures present as part of the disk's preparation for DOS operation, such as the directories or FATs and file names.

It can be forced to operate in the physical mode by starting it using the /M switch. This is particularly useful if the system areas of the disk are damaged; in this case, the information put on the disk during the low-level format is used - the side, cylinder and sector location.

Diagnostics. Within the Diagnostics program, there is a utility which carries out a range of tests on both hard and floppy disks, not unlike the early tests carried out by Calibrate. If you suspect a problem with a floppy disk, Calibrate will not be of any use and you must use the Diagnostics program.

PC Tools is currently at version 8 and also has a version for Windows.

DiskFix is a multipurpose utility which enables you to sort out and repair many disk problems on both hard and floppy disks. In functional terms, it operates at both high and low levels and combines the many of the functions of Norton Disk Doctor and Norton Calibrate. My experience of it has been quite successful and it appears to do a good job.

I find it difficult to recommend one rather than the other since they are both remarkably efficient, helpful and thoroughly useful pieces of software. Norton currently has the edge because it handles compressed drives correctly but who knows what the next version of PC Tools will come up with?   If you can afford it, get both, because the additional facilities over and above disk maintenance and data recovery are excellent.   Whichever one you decide to purchase, get the most recent version available and register it so that you will get upgrade information.   This could save you a lot of time, trouble and money.

A word about SCUZZIES, ESDIs and IDEs

Some types of hard disk - particularly those with IDE, ESDI or SCSI interfaces, use controllers which feed DOS with misleading information about the actual physical structure of the disk - these translating controllers actually modify the DOS instructions so that they fit the actual structure of the disk.   The reason for this trickery is that it is not possible for DOS to operate with the large numbers of tracks which modern drives support (often more than 1200).   These controllers allow the disks to use most features of Calibrate apart from changing the interleave.

IDE drives are quite interesting beasts - their controller cards are not conventional since most of the control logic is built into the drive. They are supplied complete with a low-level format and should never be low level formatted by the end user.   It is almost impossible to do this but some drives can be formatted by a resident utility in the computer's BIOS and this results in the complete loss of information on the affected drive.   As far as I am aware, this is only a problem with certain versions of the AMI BIOS, but it's as well to be aware of a potential hazard to your data.   It is not possible to change the interleave factor if an IDE drive (always 1:1), but pattern testing with CALIBRAT, or Spinrite is reliable enough.

CHAPTER 16
Hardware problems

Disk drives are quite complex pieces of precision electro-mechanical equipment. In spite of this, some can run for many years with no problems at all while others may die, either quietly or noisily within a few days of installation.

The most stressful times for hard disks occur when the computer is first switched on, or if they are bumped or dropped while the platters are rotating. Most hard disks fail at switch on time, and cause the POST (power- on system test) to report an error message on screen, either as a number or message. The messages are usually quite informative but the error codes (which are identical to IBM PC error codes) can be obscure unless you have a translation.

Error codes beginning with 17 are generated by MFM and RLL drives and controllers which operate with an ST506/ST412 interface; error codes beginning with 104 are given by ESDI interface drives while SCSI error codes begin with 096, 112, 113, 208, 209, 210 or 211.

Error codes are also generated if you run the IBM Advanced Diagnostics, or a similar program to diagnose a faulty machine.

The error codes and messages seem a little formidable, but, when used sensibly, they can tell you a lot about the failure and, as a result, the way in which it can be dealt with. If the controller fails, then an investigation will soon show if it has been incorrectly fitted or has any obvious problem (like, for example, overheating so that the controller starts to smell or bursts into flame!) Where the controller is suspect, replacing it with a new one is the best and usually the most practicable solution.

Where the diagnostic indicates a hard disk drive failure, you may well be able to sort it out using some of the programs and techniques mentioned in this book, but again, a new or reconditioned drive may be the best solution in the long term. Drive 0 is the first or only hard disk drive in a system and drive 1 is the second drive in a two-drive system.

Error code	Meaning
1701	Fixed disk general POST error
1702	Drive or controller time-out error
1703	Drive-seek error
1704	Controller failed
1705	Drive sector not found error
1706	Write-fault error
1707	Drive track 0 error
1708	Head-select error
1709	Error correction code (ECC) error
1710	Sector-buffer overrun
1711	Bad address mark
1712	Internal controller diagnostics failure
1713	Data-compare error
1714	Drive not ready
1715	Track 0 indicator failure
1716	Diagnostics cylinder errors
1717	Surface-read errors
1718	Hard drive type error
1720	Bad diagnostics cylinder
1726	Data-compare error
1730	Controller error
1731	Controller error
1732	Controller error
1733	BIOS undefined error return
1735	Bad command error
1736	Data-corrected error
1737	Bad track error
1738	Bad sector error

1739	Bad initialisation error
1740	Bad sense error
1750	Drive verify failure
1751	Drive read failure
1752	Drive write failure
1753	Drive random-read test failure
1754	Drive-seek test failure
1755	Controller failure
1756	Controller error-correction code (ECC) test failure
1757	Controller head-select failure
1780	Seek failure; drive 0
1781	Seek failure; drive 1
1782	Controller test failure
1790	Diagnostic cylinder read error; drive 0
1791	Diagnostic cylinder read error; drive 1

ESDI hard disk or adapter errors

Error code	Meaning
10450	Read/write test failed
10451	Read verify test failed
10452	Seek test failed
10453	Wrong device type indicated
10454	Controller test failed sector-buffer test
10455	Controller failure
10456	Controller diagnostic command failure
10461	Drive format error
10462	Controller head-select error
10463	Drive read/write sector error
10464	Drive primary defect map unreadable
10465	Controller; error correction code (ECC) 8-bit error
10466	Controller; error correction code (ECC) 9-bit error
10467	Drive soft-seek error

10468	Drive hard-seek error
10469	Drive soft-seek error count exceeded
10470	Controller-attachment diagnostic error
10471	Controller wrap mode interface error
10472	Controller wrap mode drive-select error
10473	Read verify test error
10480	Seek failure; drive 0
10481	Seek failure; drive 1
10482	Controller test failure
10483	Controller reset failure
10484	Controller head select 3 error
10485	Controller head select 3 error
10486	Controller head select 3 error
10487	Controller head select 3 error
10488	Controller read gate - command complete 2 error
10489	Controller write gate - command complete 1 error

SCSI device errors

These have 7 digits. The first 3 indicate that there is a problem with a SCSI adapter or device:

096nnnn	Adapter with 32-bit cache errors
112nnnn	Adapter, 16-bit, without cache errors
113nnnn	Mother board SCSI adapter (16 bit) errors
208nnnn	Unknown SCSI device errors
209nnnn	SCSI removable disk errors
210nnnn	SCSI hard disk errors
211nnnn	SCSI tape streamer errors

The final 'nnnn' is important since each 'n' is a digit which helps identify the problem more closely.

The first 'n' is the SCSI ID number, the second, usually the logical drive number; the third 'n' is the host adapter slot number and the fourth is an encoded version of the drive capacity. The second and fourth digits have different meanings, when, for example, the SCSI device is a CD ROM drive or a scanner.

Common Errors

The most common error I encounter is the Seek error. Usually, this is caused by incorrectly fitted data or control cables or a loose or faulty power supply or cable. It also happens if the drive select jumpers are incorrect (you sometimes find this with second-user disks). The purpose of the seek test is to see if the drive heads will move to a range of positions on the hard disk. Very occasionally, the heads will adhere to the disk platters and will not shift. This is called 'stiction' and the cure is straightforward. Hold the disk firmly and give a sharp, rotational swing, with the wrist. This usually does the trick, but is guaranteed to give the owner a few worried moments.... it will do the same to you if you drop it. This process actually frees the heads from the platters. Very occasionally, a failing power supply may give this sort of trouble since it might not be delivering enough current to the drive(s).

After the Seek error problem, the next most common is where there is an error in reading the 'diagnostics cylinder'. This could be due to wear and tear, an incorrect drive type setting, cable mistakes and, particularly with older drives, temperature-induced mistracking - one of the commonest of the intermittent errors (it doesn't appear when the drive is first switched on but may occur when it has been working for a long time).

If the drive runs roughly or irregularly, it would be sensible to check the power and other cable connectors, since these can sometimes become insecure, particularly if you have a portable machine or one which gets moved around a lot.

Hard disk controllers are usually pretty reliable; if you suspect the controller or get an error code which implicates the controller, it could be worth checking by substitution (that is, try to borrow a compatible controller) and plug it into your system. Older controllers are a bit difficult to find these days but IDE types are usually available for under £20.

If the drive, rather than the controller turns out to be the problem, you can, if you feel up to it, try swapping the drive logic board with one from an identical drive. This often works and could enable you to retrieve data from an otherwise dead unit - in fact, it is one of the methods used by firms who specialise in data recovery. The drawback is that if you were successful, you would still need a replacement drive logic board and as individual units, they are very difficult to find, let alone purchase. Unless the logic board is readily available, discard the defective drive.

CHAPTER 17
Computer viruses

A computer virus is similar, in some respects at least, to a biological virus - it invades the computer in the same way that a biological virus invades a living system and it replicates itself. Some viruses are extremely destructive to computer systems in the same way that some biological viruses are to animals and plants. Sensible PC users will try to protect their systems from attack, just as we try to avoid viral infections getting a hold on our own bodies. The important difference is, however, that computer viruses are not biological molecules. They are rogue computer programs written by misanthropic people with warped, sick or evil minds.

These viruses are often spread by the exchange of floppy disks between enthusiasts or by down-loading files from virus infected sources such as badly managed bulletin boards. Viruses have very occasionally been discovered on distribution disks of software from reputable software houses. Some viruses are relatively harmless, putting silly messages on your screen or something similar, while others can inflict serious damage to your system (and possibly your livelihood) by modifying or destroying files or even by wiping the entire hard disk clean. Some modern viruses are extremely difficult to locate and destroy because they use self-modifying code and are masters of concealment.

Viruses infect programs in several ways. Some attack executable program files and their adjuncts (the .BAT, .EXE, .COM, .SYS, .ORV and .OVL types). Some damage these files permanently by over-writing parts of them, while others attach themselves to a program and allow it to function while the virus replicates in other files. The most unpleasant viruses are those which infect the system by damaging or replacing the system files on the boot disk. These viruses can prevent the system from functioning at all, or may merely lock you out of your hard disk.

Some viruses don't show up immediately, but will wait until a triggering event takes place - such as a particular date (Friday the 13th is a case in point) or a predetermined number of file accesses. These are sometimes referred to as 'Trojan Horses'.

People worry quite a lot about viruses, but the majority of users will not have any significant problems if they adopt a code of information protection.

Briefly, this is as follows:

* If you can afford it, install a virus protection program in your system. This is essential for business users. Don't forget to buy upgrades, either by subscription or by standing order.

* Write-protect all back-up copies of software or data files.

* Be careful with whom you exchange disks or programs, particularly if you are into games playing or if you share or download data over a network or Bulletin Board (BBS).

What to look for

Virus attacks can manifest themselves in different ways - here are a few to get you worried:

* A system suddenly becomes slow or downright sluggish.

* The machine emits funny noises, such as burps, squeaks or groans.

* You get odd messages on the screen, or the screen starts behaving peculiarly with strange graphics (such as the screen 'melting').

* Programs which you use regularly suddenly start to misbehave or to fail to work properly.

* Your system refuses to boot when you switch it on.

* Files go missing (and you know you haven't erased them in a fit of panic, pique or absent mindedness).

* Executable program files start increasing in size each time that they are used (you'll only notice this if you make a note of the size of your files on a regular basis).

Not every system that shows up with one of these faults actually has a virus, but it's a good idea to check carefully if you have any doubts.

Prevention is better than cure

A number of software houses have produced good anti-virus packages. One or two are shareware, but the majority are commercial products. DOS 6 incorporates an anti virus program licensed from Central Point and this offers reasonably good protection.

Central Point have a more sophisticated Anti-Virus package, as does Norton. Dr. Solomon's Anti-Virus package is extremely good and has regular updates. These packages cost between £70 and £120 and are worth considering if you have the money and a genuine need to avoid virus-induced problems.

Mcafee offer a shareware package which includes a scanner, database and resident anti-virus program as well as a program to clean up the infection. It works well and is well supported.

There are a number of hardware anti-virus devices around which are alleged to protect against all known and future viruses. I had a brief experience with one of these devices a few months ago, but found that it was causing hardware interrupt conflicts with other parts of my system. I wasn't impressed with it, but I should stress that I didn't carry out any controlled tests, assaulting it with assorted viruses and the like. The documentation was pretty awful too so I took it out.

Arrgh! It got me!

If your system contracted a virus, the most important advice I can give you is to KEEP COOL! Don't just switch off in a panic, because it might be a false alarm and you would then lose any data that you are working on for no good reason. Take a moment to think what to do next.

If you have a good idea of the location of the virus in your system, you may be able to get rid of it quite easily by deleting affected files and replacing them from a virus-free backup.

You may have been unable to find out which programs are infected and in cases such as this you can always delete all the files on the disk and then switch off the machine. Switch on again and boot from a write-protected emergency boot disk. Reformat the hard disk and restore the files from the last backup - if you are **absolutely** sure it is virus free. This could be quite a long process if you've got a large capacity hard disk with lots of files.

There is an easier, if more costly solution. Get hold of an up-to-date copy of one of the anti-virus packages mentioned earlier in this chapter and, following the instructions, use it to find and destroy the virus and to rebuild the affected files. Then install the virus shield software so that your system is more secure against future attacks. it'll cost you a bit, but it comes cheap compared with the heart-stopping effect of some of the more recent viruses. Look upon it as insurance for the future. If you have installed a shareware anti-virus package, don't forget to register it so that the author is recompensed for their time and skill. You will also be able to receive further updates which could be extremely useful since new viruses are being discovered all the time.

Getting rid of a virus on a floppy disk is just as straightforward as it is when dealing with a virus-infected hard disk, but it's not worth bothering if you have a backup of the infected floppy.

In such cases it's safest to bin the disk.

Glossary

ABORT

To cancel or terminate a program or procedure

ACCESS TIME

The time taken for information to be called for and received. Usually relates to memory chips where the time is measured in NANOSECONDS or to HARD DISKs where the time is measured in MILLISECONDS.

ADAPTER

A circuit board and components which acts as an INTERFACE between the MOTHERBOARD and devices (such as monitors or disk drives) attached to it.

ADDRESS

A location in the computer where data or other information may be found

ARCHIVE

A name for backed up files, often saved in a compressed form to save disk space.

ARRL Advanced, Run-length Limited

A data encoding scheme for hard disks and based upon the RLL scheme. It allows nearly double the amount of information on a disk compared with about 1.5 times for RLL. Data transfer rate is a little more than 1 megabyte per second.

AT

Advanced Technology - IBM and Clone AT machines in this group use 16 or 32 bit processors, such as the 80286, 80386 or 80486.

AT HOST ADAPTER

An adapter, or system-supplied interface which provides a 40 pin interface connector, normally used with IDE (AT Interface) hard disks.

AT INTERFACE DRIVE (Also known as an IDE drive)

A type of hard disk which uses the IBM AT task file interface (40 pin) and 8- or 16-bit data transfer.   Up to two drives may be daisy-chained on the same host computer bus.   The drive can operate in a configuration which is not the same as it's physical geometry by means of a translation mode.

BACKGROUND

A process which is carried out in a way which is not visible to the user.

BACKUP

The process by which data in the form of files is copied onto another disk or tape.

BAD SECTOR

A floppy or hard disk sector which cannot hold data reliably because of damage or a manufacturing defect.

BAD TRACK TABLE

A list of CYLINDER and HEAD numbers attached to a hard disk which indicates which tracks are flawed and cannot be used reliably.   Always entered during the LOW-LEVEL FORMAT.

BBS   Bulletin Board System

A system where PCs can link up with a host system and carry out a range of activities via modems and the telephone network.   Can play havoc with the phone bills!

BIOS   Basic Input/Output System

This is found in one or two EPROMs on the motherboard of the computer, and controls the essential routines for testing the system when it is first switched on and also any other activities which involve the input or output of data, such as disk drive activities, keyboard input or video output.   Different BIOS types may be found on some of the adapter cards.

BIT

A binary digit - takes a value of 0 or 1

BOOT

A start-up sequence which loads the operating system, usually from the bootstrap or boot sector of a SYSTEM disk.   The bootstrap is a simple program in one sector of the disk, which reads in the rest of the operating system which is on the system disk.

BUFFER

A memory segment where data can be stored temporarily while it is being transferred from one device to another - such as a keyboard buffer which can store fast or irregular keystrokes and release them as required by the system.

BUG

A defect or error in a program or operating system

BUS

An electrical pathway over which power, DATA or other types of electrical signal travel.

BYTE

A number of BITS which make up a character - a byte is generally 8 bits.

CACHE

A portion of the computer's memory which is reserved for special tasks such as for holding information on disk accesses so that more commonly used files can be rapidly located. Some 80386 and 80486 CPUs have between 8 and 256kbytes of very fast cache memory built in so that they can operate very efficiently at high speeds, transferring information out to the conventional memory as required. Advanced, high capacity hard disks, and some hard disk controllers frequently have cache memory for improving data throughput.

CDROM

A circular piece of aluminised plastic, virtually identical to music CDs on which many computer programs can be stored. Currently, up to about 700 megabytes of software can be fitted in; the material can be read or copied but not altered. The CDROM is therefore a WORM! (Look it up)

CHIP

An alternative name for an integrated circuit (IC) and so called because of the small piece of silicon inside the encapsulation (generally plastic or occasionally made of a ceramic) and connecting with the outside world by means of pins for the transmission of power and data.

CLOCK

The source of the computer's timing signals and usually derived from a quartz-crystal controlled oscillator.

CLUSTER

One or more contiguous sectors on a floppy or hard disk (typically 4)

CMOS   Complementary Metal Oxide Semiconductor

A type of chip which requires very little power to operate. In AT systems, a CMOS memory chip, powered by a battery is used to store information about the system. This is known as CMOS RAM.

COMPRESSION

Removal of redundant information in files, usually by converting repetitious information into a space-saving, tokenised form. Most compression programs will compress a wide range of file types by an average of one third, although some programs claim to be able to halve the disk space taken by a program. This may be true for certain types of graphics files, but rarely of any others.

CONTROLLER

The device, usually a circuit board, which controls data transfer between the computer and it's disk drives.

CRASH In a hard disk system, the violent contact of the read/write head(s) with the magnetic media which will almost always cause damage to both.

CYLINDER (see TRACK)

DATA

Generally described as groups of facts which are processed into information which is used for communication.

DEBUG

i. A utility program contained with other DOS programs on the system disk and used for specialised purposes such as minor program amendments or tracing program execution.

ii. Detection and cure of problems in hardware or software.

DEFAULT

The assumptions the computer makes about a process if no other parameters are given. Often default parameters are placed into a program or a controller so that it carry out specific actions without user intervention.

DEFRAGMENTATION

A technique whereby fragmented files are re-organised into contiguous sequences in order to minimise access time.

DESTRUCTIVE (low level) FORMAT

A process which completely wipes original data from a disk by initialising all tracks. This is done by re-writing all track and sector information as well as all of the data areas.

DEVICE DRIVER

A program, loaded into memory and resident there which controls a non-standard device such as a specialised adapter card.

DIAGNOSTICS

A type of program which is used to analyse the operation of a computer system and normally used to detect the presence of a malfunction and to indicate in what part of the machine it has occurred.

DISK or DISC

i. A flexible plastic (usually Mylar) circle coated with a mixture of iron and other metal oxides which can be magnetised in such as way as to store data. The disk is enclosed within a protective plastic jacket and the amount of data which can be stored depends partly upon its size and the density with which the information can be stored. Known as a DISKETTE in North America. See also FLOPPY DISK. ii. Part of a HARD DISK and sometimes referred to as a PLATTER. The surfaces of the rigid aluminium disk are sputter-coated with a thin layer of magnetisable oxides. A series of such disks are enclosed in a sealed, dust-free environment to form part of the hard disk drive.

In both cases, the data is recorded onto the disk by a combined READ/WRITE HEAD, which moves across the surface on a series of tracks. On a floppy disk, the head touches the medium whereas in a HARD DISK, it travels a fraction above the surface.

DISK COMPRESSION

A clever technique whereby the capacity of a hard or floppy disk can be increased by the used of special software. The increase in capacity is often quite substantial but rarely more than double the original, uncompressed capacity. Currently, Superstor, Stacker and Doublespace are the commonest such utilities. Compressed drives sometimes cause problems when disk problems occur. DISK MAP

A graphical display of the characteristics of a floppy disk or hard disk media which would probably include details of bad sectors and other relevant information.

DOS Disk Operating System

For PCs, this is a selection of programs stored on the DOS or system disk which contain routines to permit the system to manage information provided by a user and to manage the various component parts of the computer system. It is always the first set of programs loaded into the computer before any other programs are started. PCDOS is the IBM version (provided by Microsoft) and MSDOS is Microsoft's own version and always found in non-IBM DOS machines. DOS can mean either of these types since they are very close in structure and function. DRDOS (originally from Digital Research, but now a declining part of the Novell empire) is broadly similar in what it does. Some people say that it's better than MS- or PC-DOS.....

DOS PARTITION

A logical drive which has been set up and formatted to be accepted and to operate under DOS

ECC   Error Correction Code

A series of algorithms (mathematical techniques) used to reconstruct data after the controller has exhausted it's pre-determined number of attempts to read data from a potentially faulty sector.
Usually specific to a particular type of controller. The failure of one of these to reconstruct faulty data will give rise to the Abort, Retry, Ignore, Fail message.

ESDI Enhanced Small Device Interface

A standard high speed interface for hard disks introduced in 1983. It is capable of shifting over 1 megabyte of information per second, and typically uses

an RLL controller with 34 - 60 sectors per track.
EXTENDED PARTITION

Under DOS 3.3 and more recent versions, a hard disk may have two DOS partitions. The first, from which the system can be booted is known as the primary partition and the second as the Extended partition. This partition can contain as many LOGICAL DISK VOLUMES as it will hold, each up to 32 megabytes in extent.

FAT   File Allocation Table

Two of these are constructed on each prepared (FORMATTED) floppy or hard disk and data is written to both (in case one becomes corrupted. The FAT keeps records of how much space is available on the disk and where it is located.

FILE

Information, collected together and held on disk or RAM DISK, but not in the RANDOM ACCESS MEMORY, whether conventional or extended.

FILE COMPRESSION SOFTWARE

Programs such as PKZIP, ARJ and LHARC (to name a few) which cleverly reduce the size of files so that they take up less space on the disk. The compression is reversible a required. FIRMWARE

Instructions for the computer usually found in ROM chips; a pedantic way of differentiating such material from software found on magnetic disks or tapes.

FIXED DISK - see HARD DISK

FOREGROUND

A program or operation which you see being executed on your screen.

FORMAT (HIGH-LEVEL FORMAT)

A process whereby a pattern of tracks and sectors, file allocation tables (FAT) and directory tracks are laid down on one or both sides of a magnetic disk. The process also identifies and marks defective parts of the drive media if these are present. The format can also be made to copy a system onto the disk. During the formatting process, the marking out of sectors and tracks, and the directory and FAT entries reduces the unformatted capacity to a slightly lower formatted capacity. LOW-LEVEL FORMATTING is carried out as the initial preparation of a hard disk prior to the HIGH-LEVEL FORMAT. Floppy disks have both the low and high level formats carried out simultaneously then they are formatted.

FLOPPY DISK

A circular piece of plastic, coated with a magnetisable material which can be used to store data. It is contained within a protective sleeve and is intended as a removable storage device, in contrast to a hard disk. Early floppy disks had a diameter of 8", but more recent types used on PCs have diameters of 5.25" or 3.5"; 3" disks are sometimes met with. The disk may be capable of storing data on one or both sides - currently the latter and data may be recorded in either double or high density mode. HIGH DENSITY (HD) disks are physically similar to standard density, apart from the nature of the magnetic coating which enables data to be written in a more compressed form - for 5.25" disks, this is nearly twice as densely packed as double density, whilst the 3.5" HD disks have data encoded at more than double the standard density.

FRAGMENTATION

Files which have been segmented and dispersed in several disk locations.

GIGABYTE (Gbyte)

1000 Megabytes or 1,073,741,824 bytes (a lot of bytes!)

HARD CARD

A combined 3.5" hard disk and controller mounted together on a metal plate and connected to the computer by means of the controller card. Usually met with in XT systems although modern types are available which will work in AT systems.

HARD DISK

A non-removable data storage device in which a series of flat aluminium disks coated with a magnetisable medium are spun at high speed (3600 r.p.m.) in a dust-free atmosphere. Data is written to or read from tracks using READ/WRITE HEADs in a coded form (such as MFM or RLL). Early drives had data storage capacities from as low as 2 megabytes but currently (1991) drives with capacities in excess of 300 megabytes are common. Sometimes referred to as FIXED DISKs.

HARD ERROR

The total failure of a hard drive to write to or read from a sector on the disk.

HEAD or READ/WRITE HEAD

A movable device inside a floppy drive or hard disk drive which reads, writes or erases data on the floppy disk or hard disk platter. There is one head per side of the disk or platter.

HD or HIGH DENSITY

A term used to describe floppy disks which can store data in a more compressed form than standard density disks. Data storage on disks is expressed as BITS per inch (BPI) - for 5.25 " standard (double) density disks, this is 5876 BPI compared with 9646 for high density; 3.5" double density disks can accommodate data at 8717 BPI whilst the high density types can hold 17434 BPI. The reason for this is that the HD disks have a less sensitive magnetic coating which can tolerate the high write current that is needed to produce a satisfactory result. Disks should be formatted ONLY to the capacity which the media will support, so Double Density disks should be formatted to 360k or 720k, and High Density to 1.2 megabytes or 1.44 megabytes.

HIGH-LEVEL FORMAT

See FORMAT

IDE   Integrated Drive Electronics

A type of hard disk and interface, sometimes known as the AT Interface. Sometimes also known as Intelligent Drive Electronics but it depends upon whom you talk to.

INTERFACE

A means of matching the output of one device to the input of another, usually via an adapter or protocol.

INTERLEAVE

The way in which sectors are marked on each disk track or cylinder so that the next sector to be read from or written to in sequence is ready underneath the read/write head when the system is ready to read it. The INTERLEAVE FACTOR is the ratio of the interleave to 1 - so that an interleave of 3 has a interleave factor of 3:1.

INTERMITTENT ERROR

A soft error that occurs from time to time.

JUMPER

A small connector which can be placed over two pins on a circuit board, short circuiting them. It is like a simple switch and linking two pins is the same as connecting them electrically.

KILO (K or k)

This indicates 1000 of something - in computer terms, usually refers to bytes of memory or ohms of resistance. Usually abbreviated to k or K.

KILOBIT

1000 bits

KILOBYTE

1024 bytes; sometimes referred to as 'k' or 'kByte'

LANDING ZONE

An unused track on the platters of a hard disk where the HEADs can be parked. This normally occurs when a parking program is run or an automatic parking facility is present in the disk drive. When power is shut off, the heads will come to rest on this track.

LOGICAL DRIVE

This is a drive described with a DOS letter. For example, floppy drives in a 2 drive system are usually logical drives A and B but in a single drive system, the drive can act as either drive A or drive B. This is most often applied to hard disks with capacities greater than 32 megabytes; the DOS PARTITION is logical drive C and the extended partition can have a series of logical drives (D, E etc.) which are physically part of the same hard disk.

LOW-LEVEL FORMAT

A process which prepares the platters of a hard disk for use by laying down a pattern of tracks and sectors, according to the interleave factor, with identifying information. It also marks defective sectors so that they cannot be used for data storage at a later date. Floppy disks are low-level formatted automatically as part of the FORMAT command.

M or m

An abbreviation for 1 million of something - in computing, it usually refers to the number of bytes (1,048,576 bytes is the same as 1 megabyte).

MASTER/SLAVE

This is used to define which, of two hard disks attached to the same controller card, is drive 1 (the Master) and which is drive 2 (the Slave). The setting-up of two drives normally involves moving the drive select jumpers so that the Master is drive 1 and the Slave is drive 2. Very occasionally, you may come across a 34 way hard drive cable with some of it's wires twisted between drive 1 and drive 2. In this case, both drives are set up as drive 2, in an analogous fashion to the protocol used for floppy disk drives.

MEDIUM

The magnetic material which is used to cover a disk or tape. It usually contains a mix of iron and other oxides and a binder which holds the material onto the metal or plastic base.

MEGABYTE

1,048,576 bytes

MFM   Modified Frequency Modulation

A process by which data is encoded and written to a floppy disk; also used for some hard disks.
Transfer rate for data is about 500 Kbytes per second.

NANOSECOND nS

A very small time interval, one thousand millionth of a second.

NATIVE MODE

The physical geometry of an AT Interface (IDE) drive (number of cylinders, read/write heads and sectors per track).

NATIVE/TRANSLATION MODE

This defines how an IDE drive is actually recognised by the host computer.

NON-DESTRUCTIVE (low level) FORMAT

A method by which data is temporarily read from a disk while the disk surface is initialised by the formatting process.   It is them written back to the disk which has been re-vitalised by the format.   This is a safe formatting technique.

OPERATING SYSTEM

A collection of programs which enable the computer to operate and which manage memory, data transfer and accepting information from peripherals such as the keyboard or mouse.

OPTIMISE (see de-fragmentation)

OS/2

An operating system for AT and PS/2 computers which enables multitasking on these computers and avoids the 640k memory barrier (it can address up to 16 megabytes). It also has the ability to allow a program to split itself into a number of tasks which can run concurrently, known as multi-threading. OS/2 will not work on XT computers.

OVERLAY

A program segment which is only loaded into memory when required.

PARKING

The act of moving the heads on a hard disk to the highest numbered cylinder, so that the data area is secure should the heads touch the surface of their platters during an intentional (or unintentional) move.

PARTITION

On a hard disk, a portion of the total number of tracks devoted to a single operating system, usually DOS. A hard disk can have up to 4 such partitions.

PERIPHERAL

Anything which is attached to the computer system, such as a printer, disk drive or keyboard.

PHYSICAL DRIVE

This a single floppy or hard disk drive. A hard disk (physical drive) may be divided into several LOGICAL DRIVEs, each with a drive specifier letter C:, D:, E: - for example.

PLATTER A single disk in a hard disk drive. There usually more than one, and each surface is coated with a very thin metal film (2 - 3 millionths of an inch in thickness) on which data is recorded; the surface of a platter is very smooth and flat. The heads traverse the platter 20 millionths of an inch above it's surface.... That's why you should never move a computer when it is switched on!

PORT

i. A logical address where a microprocessor can communicate with a device attached to the computer.

ii. A plug or socket which will allow a user to attach a peripheral to an adapter card.

PORT ADDRESS

A specific logical address to which an adapter may be configured so that it communicates with a computer.

POST Power On Self Test

An automatic process which starts when the computer is switched on. It will check many aspects of the computer and report on it's findings.

PRIMARY PARTITION

For Dos versions greater than 3.3, a hard disk can have two partitions which are available for DOS - a primary partition which contains the boot information, and an extended partition which can contain several logical drives.

PROGRAM

A set of coded instructions which tell the computer the method by which it should handle data or complete a task.

PUBLIC DOMAIN (Software)

Programs that are made available for free use by the author. You should only have to pay a small sum for the disk and copying charge.

RAM   Random Access Memory

Memory chips in your computer.

RAM DISK

A part of memory (conventional or extended) which is set up so that it can hold data just like a floppy disk. Because it is entirely electronic, access times are very short, but the contents of a RAM disk are lost when power is switched off. As far as DOS is concerned, a RAM disk looks like any other drive. A RAM disk is sometimes referred to as a VIRTUAL DISK.

RANDOM ACCESS FILE

This is a file in which any item of data may be read or written in any order. Each section of data is of the same length and data sections (records) are written end to end (concatenated). A record may be accessed through it's position in the file, which can be calculated from it's offset.

READ ONLY

A file which cannot be over-written until it's attribute byte has been changed.

READ-WRITE HEAD

Found on floppy and hard disk drives, this reads data from and writes data to tracks on the disk.

RLL   Run Length Limited

A type of encoding used for hard disks which encodes binary data on the platters.   More troublesome when used on cheap drives than the MFM type of encoding but can store more information for the same amount of disk space.   Generally with 26 sectors per track and capable of about 1 megabyte per second transfer rate.

ROM   Read Only Memory

A memory chip or, less correctly, a data storage device which once it is programmed, cannot be altered or erased.

ROM BIOS   Read Only Memory Basic Input/Output System

The start-up sequence for the computer is stored in this memory chip (or chips, in the case of a PC-AT).

RWC   Reduced Write Current

A technique used to decrease the intensity of the recorded signal which is transferred to magnetic media .

SCSI Small Computer Systems Interface ('Scuzzy')

A general purpose interface which operates at the system, rather than controller level (unlike ESDI, for example).   Currently usually met with in connection with hard disks but increasingly felt to be the future interface for peripherals such as CDROM drives, Scanners and similar devices.

SECTOR

Pert of one track of a floppy or hard disk which normally contains 512 bytes of data. Standard 360k and 720k floppy disks have 9 sectors per track and high density disks (1.2M and 1.44M) have 15 or 18 sectors. MFM encoded hard disks usually employ 17 sectors and RLL encoded, between 25 and 34 sectors per track, hence their greater storage ability. SEEK

The action involved in moving the read/write head of a disk drive to a given location in order to read or write data.

SELF-EXTRACTING ARCHIVE

A compressed program file that will automatically expand in size when run. As part of it's operation, it will expand any other files which were included and compressed in it when it was produced.

SEQUENTIAL FILE

One in which records are not of a fixed length but which have a delimiter between each record and the next. The data can only located as a result of a sequential search through the file.

SERVO DATA

Coded markings written on one platter of a hard disk which has a VOICE COIL ACTUATOR. These enable the read/write heads to locate each track quickly and reliably.

SHAREWARE

Computer programs which are made available to users on a 'try before you buy' basis. If you wish to continue using the programs after the trial period, you are morally obliged to send a registration fee to the author. In return, you will normally be sent an up to date and often

much better featured version of the program. Shareware may be copied and distributed but only for the cost of duplication and the disk on which it is made available.
SOFT ERROR

This occurs when a disk controller fails to read or write on it's first attempt. See Hard error and ECC.

SOFTWARE

This consists of a series of instructions which are used to direct the computer to carry out a task. Software many be written in a low-level language such as Assembler (specific to the type of microprocessor) or a high level language such as BASIC or PASCAL which is subsequently converted into a form which the computer can use directly.

ST506/412

The original standard interface used by computer hard disks and now being superseded by interfaces such as ESDI or IDE.

STEPPER MOTOR

A motor used in floppy and hard drives to move the heads across the surface of a disk by small or large amounts in a series of partial spindle rotations. The amount of rotation can be as little as 1/500 of a revolution. SYSTEM CRASH

This is usually caused by faulty software and causes the system to stop. It can only be re-started by pressing the CTRL/ALT/DEL keys, or in extreme circumstances, by pressing the reset button. It does not cause any permanent damage to the system.

SYSTEM FILES

The two files in a DOS system (IBMDOS.COM and IBMBIO.COM for PCDOS and IO.SYS and MSDOS.SYS for MSDOS) are known as system files and are hidden from a normal directory listing. Another, essential file forms the shell. This is known as COMMAND.COM in both PCDOS and MSDOS.

TPI   Tracks per inch

40 track 5.25" 360k disks have 48 TPI, 80 track 1.2M disks have 96 TPI while both types of 3.5" disk have 135 TPI. Hard disks can have track densities of 500 - 1000 TPI, hence the need for precise positioning of the read-write heads.

TRACK

A concentric circle on a disk which holds data and sometimes known as a cylinder. There are many such tracks on a disk and each holds a sequence of magnetic flux changes (domains). Data is written onto the tracks sector by sector.

TRANSLATION MODE

This is the mode (number of cylinders, sectors per track and number of read/write heads) in which an IDE (AT Interface) drive will power-up. A default mode is normally specified and can be over-ridden by the user, provided to total number of sectors required is less than the guaranteed number of sectors on the IDE drive. The number of logical heads must not exceed 17 and the number of cylinders must not exceed 1025. The number of sectors per track is usually set at 17. The product obtained by multiplying these 3 sets of figures together must not exceed the total number of guaranteed sectors on the drive.

TROJAN HORSE

An unpleasant virus which does not show its presence in your system immediately, but waits for a particular date or event.

TSR   Terminate and Stay Resident

A program which is loaded into the computer memory and remains inactive until it is called.

UNFORMATTED CAPACITY

The theoretical number of bytes which could be fitted onto a hard or floppy disk before the pattern of tracks and sectors is applied during the formatting process.   Formatting reduces this figure since sector boundaries have to be defined.

UPS   Uninterruptible Power Supply

A device, operated by high-capacity rechargeable batteries which automatically comes into effect almost instantly when the mains power supply fails.   It steps up the battery voltage to about 220 volts AC and will allow a time ranging from a few minutes to an hour or so's operation of the system.   This depends on the system which is being used and the capacity of the batteries.   The batteries are automatically re-charged when power is available.   UPS units tend to be expensive items and are normally only used where continuity of supply is essential.

UPDATE

The modification of data already in memory or in a file.

VDISK   Virtual Disk

This is synonymous with RAM DISK.

VIRUS

A program which replicates by attaching to other programs in a stealthy fashion.

VOICE COIL ACTUATOR

Found in hard disk drives, this device positions the read/write heads more rapidly than is the case with STEPPER MOTOR actuators. The necessary positioning information is written on a dedicated platter which enables the SERVO to operate with great speed and accuracy.

VOLUME

A portion of a disk which is designated by a drive specifier letter. Later versions of DOS allow the partitioning of a single hard disk into several volumes, each of which is a LOGICAL DRIVE.

VOLUME LABEL

A means of identifying a disk using a name of up to 11 characters.

WINCHESTER

Another name for a hard disk which cannot be removed from a machine in the sense that a floppy disk is removable. Sometimes referred to as a 'Winnie'; the name derives from a long-obsolete IBM drive which had 30 megabytes of fixed and 30 megabytes of removable storage. A fanciful illusion is said to have been made to the calibre of the Winchester rifle which matched this 30-30 figure.

WORM   Write Once, Read Many times

A device, usually a disk, which, once programmed can be read many times. Yes, a CDROM is one such device.

WRITE PRECOMPENSATION

A technique designed to vary the timing of signals to the read/write heads to compensate for differences in between the inner and outer tracks of a disk. Now usually met with only in connection with hard disks.

XT eXtended Technology

An early type of IBM personal computer which used an 8088 CPU and 8-bit data bus. Not very common now because of it's limited facilities.

ZIP/ZIPped

A file compression technique originated by Phil. Katz. Widely used and popular as a means of reducing the size of files so that you can get lots more on a disk.

Index

80286, 57, 148
80386, 148, 150
80486, 148, 150

ABORT, 12, 32, 147, 154
ACCESS TIME, 147, 152
ADAPTER, 119-120, 137-138, 41, 147-149, 153, 158, 163
ADDRESS, 136, 45, 56, 147, 162-163
ARCHIVE, 92, 147, 166
ARRL Advanced, Run-length Limited, 147
AT, 1, 4-7, 71-74, 76-78, 81, 83-84, 86-90, 92-94, 100-101, 106-107, 109, 111, 113, 115, 117-122, 125, 128-129, 131, 133, 135, 11, 13, 22, 25, 27-28, 31-33, 36-37, 42-43, 45, 47, 49-51, 55-56, 59, 65-66, 68, 0, 148, 150-151, 156-158, 160-162, 165, 168, 141
AT HOST ADAPTER, 148
AT INTERFACE DRIVE, 148, 168

BACKGROUND, 105, 69, 0, 148
BACKUP, 2-3, 6-7, 10, 92, 108, 114, 125, 18-19, 23, 35-36, 39-40, 49-52, 58, 60, 67-69, 148, 142, 144-145
BAD SECTOR, 104, 136, 33, 148
BAD TRACK TABLE, 148
BBS Bulletin Board System, 149

BIT, 74, 80, 87, 111, 138, 140, 16, 56, 0, 148-149, 144
BOOT, 128-129, 131, 12-13, 15-17, 21-22, 36-38, 51, 63-64, 68, 149, 163, 141, 143-144
BUS, 119-120, 148, 150, 171
BYTE, 150, 164

CACHE, 138, 150

CARTRIDGE, 49, 52
CASSETTE, 83, 105, 49
CDROM, 84, 150, 165, 170
CHIP, 101, 150-151, 165
CLOCK, 151
CLUSTER, 126, 29, 151
CMOS Complementary Metal Oxide Semiconductor, 151
CMOS RAM., 4, 8, 17, 67, 151
COERCIVITY, 71, 76, 90-91, 93, 95, 101
COMPRESSION, 1, 128, 131, 41, 63, 151, 153, 155, 171
CONTROLLER, 1-2, 5-6, 9, 72-73, 87, 95-96, 101, 106-108, 117-123, 130, 132, 134, 135-138, 140, 12, 52, 59, 151-152, 154-155, 157, 160, 165, 167
CPU, 56-57, 171
CRASH, 103-105, 126, 36, 151, 167

DATA, 1-3, 5-6, 8, 10, 71-77, 79, 81, 83-97, 99-109, 111-115, 117-123, 125-128, 130-134, 139-140, 12, 14, 23, 25-33, 35-36, 38, 45-46, 47, 49, 51-52, 55-58, 65-69, 0, 147-158, 160-166, 168-169, 171, 142, 144
DEBUG, 25, 30, 48, 152
DEFAULT, 133, 60, 152, 168
DEFRAGMENTATION, 114, 70, 152, 162
DEVICE DRIVER, 152
DIAGNOSTICS, 133, 135-136, 139, 68, 70, 0, 153
DISC, 14, 153
DISK COMPRESSION, 128, 131, 63, 153
DISK, 1-10, 71-82, 83-90, 92-96, 99-109, 111-115, 117-123, 125-134, 135-139, 11-17, 19, 21-24, 25-33, 35-46, 47, 49-52, 55-64, 65-70, 0, 147-171, 141, 144-145
DISK MAP, 153

MEDIUM, 75, 86-87, 96, 99, 103-105, 111, 125, 153, 157, 160
MEGABYTE, 90, 52, 147, 154, 160-161, 165

NANOSECOND nS, 161
NATIVE MODE, 120-121, 161
NATIVE/TRANSLATION
NICAD, 17
NON-DESTRUCTIVE

OPERATING SYSTEM, 106, 128, 12-13, 37, 55-56, 63, 0, 149-150, 154, 161-162
OVERLAY, 162

PARKING, 159, 162
PARTITION, 72, 131-132, 17, 56, 58, 154-155, 160, 162-163
PCDOS, 131, 55, 154, 168
PERIPHERAL, 162-163
PHYSICAL DRIVE
PORT ADDRESS, 163
PORT, 52, 163
POST Power On Self Test, 163
PRIMARY PARTITION, 155, 163
PROGRAM, 1, 3-5, 7, 10, 73-74, 83, 92, 96, 108, 113-114, 126, 128-130, 132-133, 135, 14, 17-18, 22, 24, 27, 29-31, 33, 35-37, 41, 43, 57-58, 60-62, 65-70, 147, 149-153, 156, 159, 162, 164, 166-167, 169-170, 141-143

RAM DISK, 83, 155, 164, 169
RAM Random Access Memory, 164
READ ONLY, 164-165
READ-WRITE HEAD, 165
RLL Run Length Limited, 87, 165
ROM Read Only Memory, 165
RWC Reduced Write Current, 165

SCANNER, 139, 69, 143

SECTOR, 1-2, 5-6, 8-9, 95, 104, 106, 109, 121-122, 127, 131-133, 136-137, 12-13, 29-33, 0, 148-149, 152, 154, 157-158, 166, 168-169
SEEK, 8-9, 117, 137-139, 166
SELF-EXTRACTING ARCHIVE, 166
SEQUENTIAL FILE, 166
SERVO DATA, 166
SHAREWARE, 125, 129-130, 39, 43-45, 47, 50, 166-167, 143-144
SOFT ERROR, 159, 167
SOFTWARE, 5, 73, 82, 85, 119, 129, 133, 18, 37, 41, 43-45, 50, 52-53, 65, 0, 150, 152-153, 155, 164, 167, 141-144
SPUTTERING, 104
STEPPER MOTOR, 6, 99, 103-104, 106-107, 130, 167, 170
SYSTEM CRASH, 167
SYSTEM FILES, 13, 16, 37, 63, 168, 141

TAPE STREAMER, 10, 138, 18, 39, 49, 52
TPI Tracks per inch, 168
TRACK, 9, 72, 79, 81, 88-91, 93-94, 96, 99-109, 117-118, 121, 123, 130, 136, 25, 35, 58, 148, 152, 155, 158-159, 161, 165-166, 168
TRANSLATION MODE, 120-121, 148, 161, 168
TROJAN HORSE, 169
TSR Terminate and Stay Resident, 169

UNFORMATTED CAPACITY, 156, 169
UPDATE, 27, 56, 169
UPS Uninterruptible Power Supply, 169

VDISK Virtual Disk, 169